# Solar Power Finance Without the Jargon

**Other Related Titles from World Scientific**

---

*The Energy Conundrum: Climate Change, Global Prosperity, and the Tough Decisions We Have to Make*
by Neil A C Hirst
ISBN: 978-1-78634-460-1
ISBN: 978-1-78634-667-4 (pbk)

*Handbook of Energy Finance: Theories, Practices and Simulations*
edited by Stéphane Goutte and Duc Khuong Nguyen
ISBN: 978-981-3278-37-0

*Metals and Energy Finance: Application of Quantitative Finance Techniques to the Evaluation of Minerals, Coal and Petroleum Projects (Second Edition)*
by Dennis L Buchanan and Mark H A Davis
ISBN: 978-1-78634-587-5
ISBN: 978-1-78634-627-8 (pbk)

*Renewable Energy Finance: Powering the Future*
edited by Charles W Donovan
ISBN: 978-1-78326-776-7
ISBN: 978-1-911299-78-3 (pbk)

# Solar Power Finance Without the Jargon

Jenny Chase

*BloombergNEF, Switzerland*

**World Scientific**

NEW JERSEY · LONDON · SINGAPORE · BEIJING · SHANGHAI · HONG KONG · TAIPEI · CHENNAI · TOKYO

*Published by*

World Scientific Publishing Europe Ltd.

57 Shelton Street, Covent Garden, London WC2H 9HE

*Head office:* 5 Toh Tuck Link, Singapore 596224

*USA office:* 27 Warren Street, Suite 401-402, Hackensack, NJ 07601

**Library of Congress Cataloging-in-Publication Data**

Names: Chase, Jenny, author.

Title: Solar power finance without the jargon / Jenny Chase (BloombergNEF, Switzerland).

Description: New Jersey : World Scientific, [2019]

Identifiers: LCCN 2019013323| ISBN 9781786347398 (hc) | ISBN 9781786347459 (pbk)

Subjects: LCSH: Solar energy industries--Finance.

Classification: LCC HD9681.A2 C43 2019 | DDC 338.4/362147--dc23

LC record available at https://lccn.loc.gov/2019013323


**British Library Cataloguing-in-Publication Data**

A catalogue record for this book is available from the British Library.

For any available supplementary material, please visit
https://www.worldscientific.com/worldscibooks/10.1142/Q0219#t=suppl

Desk Editors: Aanand Jayaraman/Jennifer Brough/Shi Ying Koe

Typeset by Stallion Press
Email: enquiries@stallionpress.com

Printed in Singapore

# About the Author

 **Jenny Chase** is the Head of the Solar Analysis team at BloombergNEF. She founded this team in 2006 at a startup called New Energy Finance, which was acquired by Bloomberg in December 2009. Now a division of Bloomberg, the firm provides market and investment research about clean energy for a primarily financial and corporate audience. Jenny leads an international team based in Hong Kong, New York, San Francisco, London and Milan to produce market research on solar power demand, supply, prices, companies and technologies. She is the main author of the quarterly *BloombergNEF PV Market Outlook*, one of the most read publications on the financials of the global solar market. Jenny holds a BSc and an MSc in Natural Sciences from the University of Cambridge, UK. She now lives in the Swiss countryside with her husband, daughter and small flock of rare breed West of England geese.

# Acknowledgements

This book is mainly collection of things I have learned from working with my colleagues, the brilliant and pleasant people of BloombergNEF. Particular thanks to Michael Liebreich, Felicia Jackson, Chris Greenwood, Xiaoyu (Julia) Wu, William Young, Francesco d'Avack, Michael Wilshire, Julia Wu, Ethan Zindler, Benjamin Kafri, Martin Simonek, Nat Bullard, Alex Toft, Pietro Radoia, Lara Hayim, Jane Swarbreck, Tom Rowlands-Rees, Colin McKerracher, Will Nelson, Yiyi Zhou, Lia Choi, John Twomey, Chris Gadomski, Jon Moore, Yali Jiang, Cecilia l'Ecluse and Dr Xiaoting Wang — but this list could have been many pages long. All of these were kind enough to add their insights to this book via interviews in summer 2018.

Thanks also to Professor Martin Green, Dr Ajay Gambhir, Belén Gallego, Morgan Bazilian, Jigar Shah, Charles Yonts, Lucy Hornby, Dr Chiara Candelise, Dr Dustin Mulvaney and Dr Zhengrong Shi.

# Contents

# Chapter 1

# Introduction

This book aims to provide a useful introduction to finance, via solar power, for people with an education in science, engineering or humanities subjects and an interest in energy technologies. It assumes very little knowledge of finance, business or economics, but fortunately none of those are difficult.

If you have an interest in such matters, you probably remember reading overexcited articles about solar power where the facts were somewhat underwhelming. Thomas Edison famously said in 1931 that he'd put his money on the sun as a source of power, but a smattering of expensive solar panels in space, on yachts, for water heating, and on calculators was presumably not what he meant. Before 2015, solar power provided less than 1% of the world's electricity, and was still heavily subsidised in most of the places it was built.

However, you may have noticed that you see a lot more solar panels around than you used to. You might see neat square rooftop solar system in the UK, a dusty panel running a streetlight in India, a solar firm name on the siding at the football World Cup, or billboards and leaflets advertising installers in the US and Australia. Almost any piece of near-future science fiction set on Earth will have a shot showing solar panels. The 2014 French film *Two Days, One Night*, starring Marion Cotillard, is about a worker being laid off from a solar panel factory in much the same way as an older film might be set around a coal mine.

This impression that there is much more solar than there used to be is not false. According to BloombergNEF data — data I have been involved in collecting since 2004 — the world had about 3.9 GW of solar panels in place at the end of 2004 and about 526 GW at the end of 2018. Total global solar investment in 2018 was $131 billion, or slightly more than the gross domestic product of Kuwait (World Bank, latest data 2017). This is actually down from $171 billion in 2017 as the price of each solar unit has fallen (this will come up again once or twice in this book), but clearly a different proposition from the $11.2 billion we recorded in 2004. When I started analysing solar in 2006, the internal joke was that my job title was Head of Improbable Technologies — solar, batteries, flywheels, hydrogen — while the real clean energy sector to watch was considered to be wind. Flywheels and hydrogen are still a little improbable, but batteries have become much cheaper and much more widely deployed, and are likely to represent a huge amount of the investment activity in energy in the next few decades.

For this book, I have drawn extensively on the work of my team and my colleagues covering other energy sectors at BloombergNEF, and on countless conversations with them. There is no better feeling than working with smart people towards a shared goal, and in this case the goal is to understand and inform our subscription clients of past and future trends in energy investment. Michael Liebreich, the founder of New Energy Finance before it was BloombergNEF and a remarkable person, was kind enough to read the chapters and directly insert some of his own insights and memories. I also conducted a series of interviews in summer 2018 with experts from academia and leading voices of the solar industry, and have included direct quotes for an additional perspective. Thank you to Professor Martin Green, Jigar Shah, Dr Ajay Gambhir, Dr Chiara Candelise, Belén Gallego, Dr Zhengrong Shi, Dustin Mulvaney, Charles Yonts and Lucy Hornby for their insight.

In general, this book takes the view that the 'how' of switching our global economy to clean energy is more interesting than the 'why'. Anthropogenic climate change is a fact, and will hit the world's poor people the hardest. Solar power is not the only or always the best solution, but it's now one of the cheapest and easiest sources of clean energy and is likely to have a significant impact, particularly in sunny countries. Some chapters draw sceptical conclusions about the economic efficiency or fairness of certain policies to support solar industry growth, even the ones which worked. To solve the problem of climate change, we need to be clever as well as enthusiastic.

While much progress has been made and the last 14 years have been very interesting times to work in solar, the excitement is not yet over. Solar is still only about 2% of electricity generation worldwide, though above 8% in certain countries and growing very rapidly indeed. We are only beginning to figure out how cheap energy that is only available at certain times affects the economic and ecological trade-offs our civilisation makes for power. Questions (and disinformation) about pricing, intermittency, the cost and necessity of backup generation and what solar can actually do are likely to become much more mainstream. This book will explain the basic concepts you need to know about, which will still be useful to know when the data here on solar cost and penetration are tragically out of date, which they will be. My team's day job at Bloomberg is to maintain monthly, if not weekly, pricing information and short-term forecasts.

There will be plenty of work, and good decisions needing to be made, in this sector in our lifetimes for smart people who understand the basics of solar, power markets and finance. I hope this book provides an easily readable introduction.

# Chapter 2

# Solar Technologies — The Basics

There are three major applications for solar power. They are passive solar heating, solar thermal electricity generation and photovoltaics. The first two involve using the sun's heat to make a fluid — usually water — hot, and if you make it very hot you can use the steam to run a turbine to generate electricity, exactly as in fossil fuel-fired power plants. They are included for completeness and because solar heat can, in the right place, significantly contribute to energy supply. The third application, photovoltaics, is the main focus of this book. It is a technology that has no moving parts and requires no material inputs once it is installed, and generates electricity directly. It is also the one that has made great progress technically and economically in the last few decades, and looks set to explode further.

## 2.1. A Note on Units

Anyone interested in energy markets should first have a good, intuitive grip on basic school physics regarding power and energy. This is too important, and too frequently poorly understood, to put in an appendix. Energy is the simpler of these concepts, and refers to the potential to do work — to move a weight, or illuminate a light bulb for a period of time, or heat a volume of water. The scientific unit for energy is a joule (4.18 J make a calorie, but a calorie is a unit now seldom used outside food science). A joule is a derived unit of more fundamental metrics, but basically 10 J is roughly enough to lift 1 kg a distance of 1 m in Earth gravity.

When we discuss electrical energy and power, we usually use watts (W) and watt-hours (Wh). Power is the rate of delivery of energy, and measured in W, where $1\,W = 1\,J/s$. A lightbulb with a power rating of 28 W uses 28 J/s while it is switched on. To measure how much energy it uses over the day, we multiply the power by the time, i.e. watts × seconds. A 28 W lightbulb running for an hour uses $28 \times 60 \times 60\,Ws$ or, as we would normally write it, 28 Wh. A cup of tea (say 250 mL) requires about 24 Wh to boil if it starts at 20°C and the kettle boils exactly the right amount (making anything hot is surprisingly energy-intensive). Wh convert directly into joules, but are generally more intuitive units for electrical energy. In practice, we more often speak of energy delivered in kWh (kilo, k = a thousand), MWh (mega, M = a million) or even GWh (giga, G = a thousand million) or TWh (tera, T = a million million). When we speak of a power rating for a generating plant, it is usually rated in kW, MW or even GW if it is large — which indicates the power it will generate under good conditions. A coal power generation plant is 1–4 GW. A power output of 1 GW would boil an Olympic sized swimming pool starting at 20°C in about 14 min. A solar plant covering two or three hectares is roughly 1 MW, so a solar plant with peak power capacity of 1 GW would cover about 3,500 football pitches. The actual expected energy from these will be discussed later; obviously, the solar plant will generate only when the sun is shining, and then often not at full capacity, while the coal plant can to some extent be ramped up and down as needed.

When we discuss electricity prices, we usually talk about them by the kWh for households (the average annual electricity consumption of a European house is a few thousand kWh), and by the MWh for bulk electricity sales. A typical price for electricity sold to a European household is 15–30 eurocents/kWh, in the UK 12–15 per kWh and in the US prices range from about 11 cents (in Southern states) to about 30 cents (in California or Hawaii) per kWh. I will generally use dollars throughout this text even for prices in non-US countries, as most of the world is aware of approximately what a dollar is worth, and it will save giving a long list of currency conversions which will inevitably miss out important ones.

When electricity is sold in bulk, a low price might be $30/MWh, while $200/MWh would be considered a high price and probably correspond to an unusual situation, such as power being generated by burning expensive diesel fuel.

Another unit worth being aware of is the tonne of oil equivalent (toe), a unit used when electricity, heat and transport fuel are being compared together as 'gross (or primary) energy supply' by bodies such as the International Energy Agency (IEA) which historically focus on energy availability. A toe is 41.868 GJ (a standard measure, since grades of oil have slightly different energy content), or, using the simple conversion that 1 W is 1 J/s, 11.6 MWh.

This, as used by the IEA, can be very misleading when applied to renewables. The methodology for calculating primary energy consumption counts input energy — for example, an oil fired power plant literally burns tonnes of oil to produce electricity — rather than useful energy. Oil fired power plants have conversion efficiencies of 30–45%, and the contribution of oil to the electricity supply looks larger when the power plant is less efficient. A direct electrical generation plant such as solar, wind or hydro would be recorded at only its actual electrical contribution. This has the effect of making 100 MWh generated by an oil-fired power plant with efficiency 33% look three times as important to energy supply as 100 MWh generated by solar, which is nonsense. Similar calculations apply to coal and gas. An IEA report published in July 2008 pegged the global average efficiencies of electricity production at 34% for coal, 37% for oil and 40% for natural gas.

This seems like a trivial definition point, and for the IEA it probably is, because the IEA understands it. Primary energy consumption/supply should be interpreted to compare how *dependent* a country (or other entity) is on different energy sources, not to measure their contribution. Oil company BP presents the data in a different way, assuming a thermal combustion efficiency to 'uprate' renewable energy to the fossil energy it displaces in its Statistical Review of Global Energy (which is now more widely cited than the IEA statistics, probably because it is available for free).

A typical example of primary energy consumption used to denigrate the contribution of renewables was a Spectator feature published on May 13, 2017, less-than-neutrally entitled *Wind turbines are neither clean nor green and they provide zero global energy*, states that "to the nearest whole number, there is still no wind power on Earth.... From the International Energy Agency's 2016 Key Renewables Trends, we can see that wind provided 0.46% of global energy consumption in 2014".

The BP Statistical Review, which adjusts so as not to count wasted heat in power generation as useful energy, has wind energy at 1.2% of global energy consumption in 2014 — which isn't a lot, but completely negates the point of the article. (It rose to 1.9% in 2017. Solar, according to BP, was 0.35% of world energy consumption in 2014 and 0.74% in 2017.)

British Thermal Units are sometimes used instead of tonnes of oil equivalent as a measure of how much bulk energy goes into the system, and have the same consequence of making less efficient fuel conversion methods look more significant.

## 2.2. Passive Solar Heating

Solar thermal technologies will not be the main topic of this book, as photovoltaics is now the dominant solar technology. For completeness, let's start with the oldest and simplest — using the sun to heat substances (usually water) to a temperature below boiling point.

Passive solar water heating can be incredibly useful in saving fossil fuel, but it's essentially just a set of black tubes that you place in the sun and pump water through. Some improvements are possible — vacuum tubes can be used to make the water heating more efficient, for example — and it has a place in heating water up to about 80°C for washing, swimming pools and other everyday uses. Since it takes as much energy to heat water from 20°C to 30°C as it takes to heat water from 70° to 80°C, it can make a major difference in the total cost/carbon emissions of having a hot shower even in relatively cool climates, but it is unlikely to completely change the world's energy mix. Basic, cheap solar water heating systems like those in Figure 2.1 are to be found on many roofs in China, Israel and Greece. Although these simply use convection to circulate hot water into the tank and bring up cool water, more complex systems using pumps and thermostats are available and more likely to be used in cooler climates where some additional heating is often required.

Solar passive heating is also a term sometimes used for designing houses for warmth, for example by putting large windows on the south side of houses in northern Europe to maximise the warming effect of winter sun, while keeping north-facing windows small to improve insulation.

Figure 2.1.   A simple thermosiphon home solar water heating system.
*Source*: Shutterstock.

## 2.3. Solar Thermal Electricity Generation

Solar thermal electricity generation (aka Concentrated Solar Power, CSP) is where vast fields of mirrors are used to concentrate solar heat on receiver tubes or boilers full of fluid to reach temperatures up to 600°C, producing steam to drive turbines to produce electricity. This sounds promising, but ultimately is probably too expensive to revolutionise the world's energy mix. The first solar thermal electricity plants built in the late 1980s in Kramer Junction, California, and at peak generate 350 MW of power. A crash in the price of gas drove the owner into bankruptcy, but the plants were bought at a discount and as of 2015 are still in operation.

Gigawatts of solar thermal capacity were deployed from 2007 to 2014, mainly in Spain and the US, and these plants are functioning well enough — but as of early 2018, the cheapest anyone has signed a power price agreement and actually built the project without substantial additional subsidy is $138/MWh (for the Nooro Phase II and III complex in

Ouarzazate, Morocco) versus well under $40/MWh for photovoltaics. A 200 MW project in Dubai in 2017 has proposed $94.5/MWh, but is not due to be built until 2021, and is probably an outlier where the primary purpose of the builder is not to make money (developer ACWA later reported a levelised cost of energy (LCOE) of $73/MWh for the expanded 700 MW project, but as Chapter 14 will explain, never trust a LCOE unless you can see all the assumptions). A project in Australia, Aurora, was offered a price of $61/MWh by the government, but was cancelled in April 2019 after the developer failed to find any investors willing to take the risk.

Solar thermal electricity generation has a few advantages over photovoltaics — the power generation is much more stable, as the system has thermal inertia and the turbine will keep spinning for up to half an hour after the sun goes behind a cloud; and the heat can be stored in tanks of molten salt (which is then used to make the steam which pushes turbines round when the sun has gone down), or supplemented by burning gas, coal or oil. Most solar thermal electricity plants burn at least a little gas to get the boiler up to temperature in the morning, and with a big enough mirror field and tank of hot salt, the plant can even run all night and provide baseload. Molten salt is not fun to work with; if it cools off in pipes to a chilly ~270°C, it will turn solid and become tremendously difficult to extract, and when molten it has a habit of leaking out. Another reason why a truly baseload solar thermal plant is not usually economically effective is that power demand is low at night. Most North African and Middle Eastern economies have a power demand peak in the early evening, around 5–8 pm, when factories and air conditioning are still running but people also come home and start to cook dinner or watch television. This is well after the daily generation peak for photovoltaics, which is generally 10 am–3 pm; after this time, the sun is low in the sky and delivers little energy, for reasons which are apparent if you shine a spotlight torch onto a globe. When the light is coming in at an angle, the same light is spread over a much larger patch.

One effective configuration is to use enough salt and mirrors to store energy to run the plant for about four hours after sunset, covering the evening demand peak but not paying the extra to run overnight. In March 2014, the South African government agreed to pay solar thermal plants 270%

Figure 2.2.   A parabolic trough solar thermal plant.
*Source*: Shutterstock.

more for power delivered for five hours in the late afternoon and evening — when it is in demand. The beauty of solar thermal is that plants can be individually tailored to deliver power when it is most optimal — but this is their flaw as well, for solar thermal plants cannot be standardised and mass-produced cheaply as photovoltaics can. Turbines and boilers are expensive, and engineering for each site and schedule is more so. At present, it seems likely that solar thermal electricity generation will only be deployed in countries with weak grids and those with a strong evening peak, and will ultimately lose to photovoltaics and batteries.

There are two major types of solar thermal electricity generation, parabolic trough and tower and heliostat (Figure 2.2). These will be discussed further in Chapter 17.

## 2.4.  Photovoltaics

The last and most exciting type of solar is photovoltaics, a family of technologies which use light falling on certain materials ('semiconductors') to produce an electrical current. A photovoltaic module is a sandwich of glass, semiconductor, silver paste to act as an electrical contact, and materials to stop the water getting in (water ruins semiconductors). Chapter 18

Figure 2.3.    Ordinary crystalline silicon modules installed on a roof.
*Source*: Shutterstock.

will go into more detail about the types of semiconductor which can be used, and their advantages and disadvantages (Figure 2.3).

A solar module produces direct current (DC) — straightforwardly, electric current only flows one way out of it. Most modern devices and most grids, however, run on alternating current (AC) — an electric current that reverses direction many times per second. The reason we use AC in our grids is that the alternation makes it possible to use very high voltages in long distance transmission lines, which is more efficient than using low voltages, and 'step down' to lower voltages which can be used safely in our homes. It is relatively difficult to change the voltage of DC power without first changing it to AC power and back.

A solar module is electrically wired into an inverter, a device which transforms the DC produced by the solar module into the AC used by the grid. A major trend of the next 20 years will probably be for televisions and refrigerators which run off direct current and are highly efficient, designed to run off a solar panel and a battery in places without grid.

The AC capacity of a system is the capacity of its inverter; the DC capacity is that of its modules.

Photovoltaic modules are essentially a commodity, which in economics means a marketable item that is not differentiated. Commodities might include copper and wheat, where you specify a certain quality and then one tonne is much like another. Cars, computers and clothes are not commodities; people tend to value certain of these well above others, often for personal reasons. The reason for drawing this distinction between 'commodities' and 'not commodities' is that I am often asked which photovoltaic modules are 'best', and the truth is, as long as a module is not fundamentally badly manufactured, there are few reasons to have a strong preference. The output of a module is measured in W, and modules are priced per W. This is the amount of power produced by the module under standard test conditions — a temperature of 25°C and incoming sunlight of 1000 W/m$^2$. This corresponds roughly to a sunny noon in Spain. In real world conditions, PV panels will be producing their rated wattage only rarely in less sunny countries.

The actual energy produced by the module (in Wh or kWh) is a function of its rated wattage and how sunny a place it is installed, and is usually expressed as a capacity factor percentage. This is the energy produced per year in Wh, divided by the W rating of the module, divided by the number of hours in a year. Imagine that the module produces either at peak power or not at all; the capacity factor is the percentage of the year it would be generating to produce the same amount of energy as it actually produces. Capacity factors for photovoltaics are not high; of course they can never be over 50%, because it's dark half the time. They are typically around 11–12% in Germany, rising to 23–25% in the Atacama Desert in Chile, or up to 35% if the panels are mounted on a tracking system to follow the sun. All capacity factors here are expressed as a function of the direct current rating of the modules. An alternative is to use the maximum output of the inverter, which gives a higher value in most configurations and is referred to as the alternating current (AC) capacity. If you see higher capacity factors for a photovoltaic plant, they are probably AC capacity factors. There is more detail on AC versus DC capacity factors in Section 18.3 of Chapter 18.

We have not mentioned efficiency, which is a red herring in popular understanding of photovoltaics — you will often see the claim that photovoltaics 'need to get more efficient to be useful'. This is not true. Efficiency is a measure of the useful energy coming out of a generator, divided by the energy in. In photovoltaics, the energy in comes from the sun and does not cost anything, so although the efficiency of standard modules on the market is only around 17–18%, that merely means they are wasting sunlight. The main difference between high efficiency and low efficiency modules is the space they take up, and we are not running out of roof or desert any time soon. 'How much does it cost?' is a more important first question than 'how efficient is it?'

Of course, higher efficiency is desirable. The cost to install and wire up a 300 W module is about the same as for a 150 W module of the same physical size, and sometimes space is limited. Module manufacturers also try to tweak their 'recipe' for greater efficiency using the same materials, which increases their profit margin since modules are sold on a per-W basis. There are also occasional attempts to sell very low efficiency photovoltaic modules (below 8%) as 'building-integrated' products installed instead of glass or a roofing material, but generally this is an architectural gimmick, and since they are usually installed without reference to where the sun will be, they are probably not worth the trouble of wiring up. They are also usually the modules that the manufacturer can't flog to a discerning buyer who is more concerned with how much they generate than how they look.

'Quality' in photovoltaic modules is something different to 'efficiency'. A photovoltaic module is under warranty for at least 25 years, after which it should still be producing at 80% of its original output. However, the buyer does not want to have to claim on the warranty, mainly because the manufacturer is likely to go bankrupt long before this (see Chapter 13). The buyer needs to know that the module has been manufactured properly, without cutting corners or using materials not tested for the whole lifetime.

There is another standard for modules, which is bankability. Banks are lazy, or, to be more specific, they cannot spend the time doing a lot of research for every loan they make (or they would make fewer loans, and charge the borrowers higher fees). Banks therefore take information shortcuts. One of these is to consider technical due diligence reports on only a few of the solar module brands on the market, rather than read 500+ different pleas for consideration. This means that they are much more likely to finance a project using modules that they have looked at before. A module is 'bankable' if a bank can be expected to have heard of and looked at the brand.

These features are pretty much independent of the semiconductor used, although as of 2018, about 96% of the modules on the market are crystalline silicon, with the remainder thin-film cadmium telluride or copper indium gallium selenide.

There will still be attempts to develop a 'black swan' technology. A black swan is something that is significant, but could not have been predicted. Originally the term was a phrase used in Europe, possibly since very ancient times, to describe something impossible as the swan species found in Europe are all white. Then European explorers discovered a species of black swan in Australia, and the phrase acquired the meaning it has today. Obviously, I cannot rule out a black swan technology in photovoltaics, but neither can I predict it, by the very definition of a black swan.

Perovskites, a family of lead compound semiconductors, are currently the front runner for a black swan/rapid, market-changing breakthrough in photovoltaic module technology. Perovskites have improved efficiency very rapidly in the lab, above 20%, and may be suitable for applying as a second layer on top of conventional crystalline silicon wafers. However, current laboratory attempts to make a perovskite cell degrade significantly in 5 years, which given ordinary modules are under warranty for 80% of their initial capacity for 25 years, is not attractive.

# Chapter 3

# Startups

## 3.1. What Is a Startup?

A startup is a brand new company created by one or more founders who put money and time into the organisation. Usually the term is used for companies that have ambition to become very large, rather than, for example, a new restaurant or small trading house which may target a small steady profit for the owners but is unlikely to grow rapidly. Although the stereotype of a startup is three recent graduates working in a garage, most successful startups are organised by experienced people who spot a gap in a market they know well. There are also 'serial entrepreneurs' who make a habit of spotting a market gap and spend a few years at a time creating companies to fill it. (Michael Liebreich, founder of New Energy Finance, is both an experienced person who spotted a gap in the market, and a serial entrepreneur.) Although I cannot cite academic literature on this, it seems safe to say that startups founded by experienced people are more likely to succeed than those attempted by recent college graduates.

The founders of a startup own shares in the company jointly (a share is a small portion of a company, and these exist for private companies as well as those on public markets), and initially work on figuring out how their company could one day make money. If it is a simple concept and doesn't require much capital, they may have enough of their own money to get to profitability, but usually this is not possible. If they need more funds than they can provide, they may raise money from 'friends and family' or 'angels' i.e. rich people — or, if they need more, they seek a 'venture capital (VC) investor' and sell a stake in the company in exchange for cash that the company uses to develop the product and service. The founders may do this several times, and if the investor is satisfied that the value of the business is growing with the additional money put into it, they may increase their stake (sometimes at a higher valuation, i.e. paying more per share, if they think that the founders have in the meantime made the company more valuable, for instance by increasing revenues or attracting a number of new users).

The ultimate aim of this is to achieve an 'investor exit', where all those who have put in money sell the shares that they have accumulated for more than they paid for them, and the founders sell at least some of their own shares and turn them into cash. Founders normally have a form of 'lock-in period' on most of their shares, to encourage them to stay around and work towards the ambitious growth plan they presented to whoever is buying the company. The lock-in period prohibits founders from selling (most of) their shares immediately, and there is usually an 'earn-out' period during which the acquired company is expected to meet certain performance metrics.

An investor exit might be an Initial Public Offering (IPO), where a company lists its shares on the stock market and a different sort of investor, one that likes to own and trade publicly listed shares, can buy them. Or the startup might be bought by another firm for its technology, its people, or its business, called a 'strategic exit'. Famous strategic exits include Yahoo's purchase of Tumblr for $1.1 billion in 2013, and Microsoft's acquisition of Linkedin for $26 billion in 2016. A major solar exit was the IPO of German solar cell maker Q-Cells in 2005, which made some of its investors enormous returns — Apax, for example, reportedly received EUR 277 million ($334 million) from its investment of EUR 11.5 million just a year earlier. A much less famous example is the acquisition of my company, New Energy Finance, by Bloomberg in December 2009. This was considered successful by our angel and VC investors and by the staff who had received stock options. I spent my share of the proceeds on a garden.

The VC investor anticipates a high failure rate. Assessing the risk is the job of venture capitalists, and the failure rate is the reason they need to earn a massive profit from the few really big successes. VCs are often criticised for wanting a very high return on their investment, mainly by founders who can't raise money at the valuation they think their business deserves. Generally, if you can make your business a success without giving up a stake to VCs, it makes sense to do so. But many businesses really need the money in the early stages, and could not reach profitability without it.

## 3.2. Startup Failure Rates

Failure is far more common in investment than I would have expected as a physics graduate. While it's difficult to put a precise figure on it due to questions about what counts as a 'startup' and what counts as 'failure', it is generally estimated that 70–75% of startups fail (the Kauffman Institute, which studies US startup activity, found in 2016 that 48.7% of new businesses tracked reached their fifth year of operation).

Many that do not fail will barely scrape a profit, and the VC investor lives by the occasional big success. I estimate that about half of all the businesses I have written about in my 12-year career have gone bankrupt or ceased activities in solar power, even the big ones with hundreds of employees — and a much higher proportion of the startups.

Out of curiosity about whether this is the case in other sectors, I took the 2010 Global Top 100 Awards list of US VC publication Red Herring, and tried to find out where they are as of late 2018. Thanks to Google, this is not difficult to do approximately, although there will of course be subtleties. The first surprise about the Red Herring Global Top 100 Award Winners 2010 is that there are 102 of them.

Figure 3.1 shows the results. Initial Public Offerings (IPOs) are easy to spot — a company once listed on the stock market becomes much more visible to a quick Google search — and probably represent the best outcome for investors, as a startup company must grow considerably to be eligible for a public offering. The four IPOs among the Red Herring 2010 winners included Israeli–US solar panel-level optimiser company maker SolarEdge, which listed on the US Nasdaq in March 2015. Merger and acquisition (M&A) deals are not much more difficult to find, although it's nearly impossible to identify which were highly profitable and which are simply investors cutting their losses. I did not count those where the

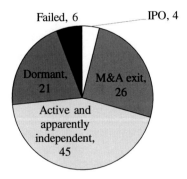

Figure 3.1.   Status of Red Herring Global Top 100 Award Winners 2010, as of an internet search by the author in late 2018.

coverage of their acquisition specified that the company had already failed and assets were being picked up by another firm, presumably for a negligible amount of money.

The next category is those still active (i.e. with a recently updated website, or recent press coverage), but which had not yet had an investor exit — perhaps the time is not right, but after 8 years, the investors may already feel that this has tied up their capital for too long. A further 21 companies were dormant, i.e. they had not updated their website for several years, or no longer had a website; and six, mainly US-based, had an actual paper trail of failure. It is likely that many of the dormant firms had failed, but understandably neither investors nor founders like to publicise this fact, and there is not always media interest in digging into the failure of a small and obscure private company.

Only 74% of the winners of a reasonably prestigious award are still around 8 years later. It is impossible to know in most cases if they have achieved profitability, and some may still be raising more rounds of VC on the strength of increasing client base or revenues.

# Chapter 4

# Startups: Case Study of a Startup (BloombergNEF)

After a more general chapter about startups, I'd like to share my experience of being part of a successful one, from very early on to its profitable acquisition and integration into a larger company. Most startups will not succeed, and I was very lucky to be part of one that did. Nonetheless, the experience of working there would have been worthwhile even if it had failed, for anyone with few responsibilities and a lot to learn.

This chapter is not pitched at people who have always wanted to join or found a startup, and know all about small, fast-growing organisations. Skip this chapter if you are already planning your stock option negotiation opener.

## 4.1. The Early Days

In the summer of 2004, I was cleaning windows during the holidays from studying physics at Cambridge, where I'd learned that lots of people are smarter than me. I wanted to get a job in clean energy when I graduated, but my CV was somewhat sparse on relevant experience — I'd stacked wood, delivered papers, and washed dishes in a local pub. So when an internship came up in renewable energy data entry in London at 10 pounds a day I applied, and went off on the train to interview, wearing my mum's blazer.

The company was called New Energy Finance and the website had looked professional to me. Apparently a lot of the format code was lifted from a florist's website by the Polish programmer. My first interview, with editor Felicia Jackson, consisted of a lot of garbled enthusiasm on my part and my admission that I didn't have my own laptop computer to bring in and work on. My application was rejected, and I went back to cleaning windows (it was a pretty good gig at six pounds an hour for reasonably pleasant outdoors work with a nice boss).

A few weeks later, Felicia contacted me saying that someone else had dropped out of their internship program and a spare computer was available, if I still wanted to try for a few weeks. I did. I set off for London, moved in with an unsuitable boyfriend and bought an Underground travelcard.

The team consisted of founders Michael Liebreich and Bozkurt Aydinoglu, Felicia and two or three interns, in the boardroom of a friend of Michael's. We had a water cooler and that was it for refreshments; just as well since there was a single toilet used by the entire building. What we were doing was removing superlatives from press releases to turn them into news articles (journalism!) and adding companies, renewable energy projects and financial transactions to a database Michael and Boz had designed. They thought that there were maybe 800 companies in renewable energy worldwide. We quickly discovered a lot more than that. Last time I checked we were tracking over 25,000.

Most of these companies are legitimate, but there was and is a shocking amount of suspicious behaviour that is borderline or properly fraudulent. The classic example is the 'pump and dump scam', now rare on the major stock markets of the world but still found on the minor 'over the counter' (OTC) stock markets. These OTC markets are lightly regulated and do not require companies to submit very thoroughly audited reports. They can be a route for young companies to raise money from a large pool of investors and to raise their profile, helping them commercialise their product or idea. Investors, meanwhile, can take a small punt on an interesting firm. The companies are generally still majority-owned by their management, and unlike on the major stock markets, get away with a lot of poetic license in what they release (the positive way of putting it is 'the over the counter markets are not shackled by excessive regulation'). It is normal for a very young company to have little or no revenue, and sometimes a grand plan to build a better mousetrap will actually pay off. There are legitimate companies on over-the-counter stock markets, genuinely trying to start a new and risky business with investor money.

There are also scams. One example I began, in 2005, by taking seriously was a company that had access to a large area of forest in Canada devastated by the mountain pine beetle. Since the trees were dead, the company planned to remove them and ship the wood to Europe, selling it as fuel for power plants, which would help European countries meet their renewable energy targets. The company regularly announced that it was on the brink of signing a contract worth hundreds of millions of dollars for this beetle-killed wood. The wording would suggest that the deal was practically done. This would increase the stock price, as naïve investors bought in. I assume that the management would then quietly sell some shares. Of course, nothing more would ever be said of the contract and it is probably safe to say that no dead trees were ever removed.

As an innocent journalist/researcher, I obviously wanted to cover the company properly, and would frequently ring the number in the press release for an update on the contract. Finally, I was asked gruffly, 'What are you trying to do — catch me out?'. I started to dimly realise that not all people with green plans are entirely honest. An experienced journalist would have realised immediately that the company was either uninteresting or fraudulent, and ignored it. The company had yet to close a contract as of late 2018.

Michael Liebreich's company New Energy Finance might easily have been one of those firms that were not quite on the level. Michael was a dot com entrepreneur who had ridden the boom all the way up and almost all the way back down; he had seen a vast paper fortune turn to almost nothing — though he was still richer than anyone else I knew — and was rolling the dice so he didn't have to go back to being a management consultant. He and his friend Bozkurt had decided in late 2003 to see if there was any substance behind the 'hydrogen economy' hype that was sweeping the business bookshelf at airports around the world; they had decided there probably wasn't. In the process, however, they had spotted two things others had missed: that renewable energy was on the move, and that there was a dire lack of the sort of information that investors would need. There were plenty of words written about renewable energy by credulous enthusiasts, academic papers on the workings of technology, and policy papers coming out of odd corners of governments, but very little attempt to really size or define the market, analyse the economics or think about where the money would come from. The narrative was that governments had to subsidise all renewable energy technologies, but there was little realistic projection of how long this would be necessary. The standard answer of the clean energy industry to 'what do we want?' was always 'more subsidies!'

We still see this mindset — that renewable energy companies need and deserve endless subsidy and charity — but it is changing. The reason for this has nothing to do with oil prices or gas prices or increases in power bills. It's simply that solar panels and wind turbines are now vastly cheaper than they were. All those subsidies worked — companies did drive down costs and improve their products — but we will get back to that. Back in 2004 there was little good information about how much these technologies cost or how they were being funded, and by whom.

So the idea was to build a big database and sell subscriptions to investors, who would like to read about themselves and about opportunities to invest, and be able to track down others with an interest in the sector. Michael's cunning plan was to use starry-eyed interns earning 10 pounds a day to collect and enter this data, a model Michael had used at his first startup (a skiing website called Ifyouski.com; he points out that as of 2018 you can still visit it and book a holiday). Incidentally, Michael comes out quite badly from this brief description, but it will hopefully become obvious that he created considerable opportunities for those early interns; for many of us, it was the start of a career we love, and most of the others had a great time and learned a lot. As soon as it raised some money New Energy Finance switched to reasonably-paid internships, accessible to people who can't afford to live in major cities unpaid for months.

I was one of the earliest of these interns, and I must have done something right because Michael said I should come back and work for him when I graduated. He probably meant it as a joke. I started focusing on my studies for my final year, and achieved the remarkably useless feat of improving my position from the worst 2.2 in the year to the best 2.2 in the year. Fortunately, it never crossed Michael's mind that one of his hires could fail to get a top degree, as he had, and he never asked. (This caused some embarrassment years later when he introduced me to a crowd of potential clients as someone with a First class degree in theoretical physics from Cambridge. There are few good times to correct your boss on something like that, and that wasn't one of them, so his illusion persisted for several more years.)

New Energy Finance survived, and ten days after graduation in summer 2005 I went back to work for Michael and NEF for the grand sum of 17,000 pounds a year, which washes a lot of windows. I have no idea how that compares to market rates in London at the time, but the unsuitable boyfriend was earning 22,000 pounds as a programmer. My first paycheck was unbankable because Michael had forgotten to sign it (he did very promptly when this was pointed out), and I wasn't leaving the office before 9 pm, but I was learning — something I badly needed to do.

I spent my first six months at New Energy Finance covering general clean energy news and data entry, which I really recommend as a way to learn about a subject. Journalists aren't expected to know a lot, which is why they can go around asking questions which seem stupid to experts (good journalists don't remain ignorant for long, but they keep asking the questions).

We were, like nearly all startups, not profitable, and I knew that we relied monthly on our CEO Michael Liebreich paying us out of his savings, and later on raising regular investment rounds. It was only afterwards that I heard the stories about how close to the brink we had been for the first couple of years. Michael now tells the story about how he closed the first round of external funding on January 17, 2006, with payroll due on January 26, no money in the bank, no savings, and no plan B in case the deal fell through. (As soon as he sold the company, the first thing he did was pay his debts to American Express and his brother-in-law.)

Fortunately, I had no financial responsibilities, and had we closed down, I would have given the required month's notice on my rent and moved back in with my parents in the countryside while applying for other jobs around the country and cleaning windows. I admire that Michael managed to impart continual confidence in the company's prospects, even when he must have been sweating about the imminent need to close the funding round, without ever making false promises or encouraging a false sense of security. An important property of a CEO is the ability to instil confidence in the company's future, while an important property of a startup employee is a plan to avoid homelessness in case the company folds and further salary is not forthcoming. This is tough on people without support networks or a financial safety net. I don't know what the solution is for everyone, but for me it was reassuring to rent through London's extensive informal house sharing economy, so as not to be locked into a long term contract. Working for a startup is a difficult option for the settled.

Michael awarded 'stock options' to loyal staff quite early on, prompting me to an internet search to figure out what they are. Stock options are a right to purchase shares in the company at a fixed price, normally the price of shares in the latest venture round at the time the stock option is awarded. The options do not have to be exercised (i.e. the shares do not need to be bought, and usually can't be) until an investor exit. They are therefore worthless at the time they are awarded, and will be completely worthless unless the company succeeds. They are a way to reward employees without burning cash that would be better invested in the business. However, if an investor exit is achieved, it is likely that the per-share price will be much higher and therefore the employees will get a bonus, possibly quite a significant one. As an employee it therefore makes sense to ask for as many stock options as possible if you believe the startup will be successful — and if you don't believe it will be successful, why are you there?

I was, obviously, surprised to get some stock options and would not have known to ask for them. Michael was scrupulously fair and generous on this point (perhaps I could have negotiated for more, but it probably would have been greedy).

Another thing that Michael always encourages founders to do is formalise the legal ownership of the company early, even if everyone involved is a friend or an intern. This might seem unnecessary before the company even has real existence, but venture capital investors need the ownership situation to be crystal clear before they even consider taking a stake, and arguments can get extremely acrimonious if the company is a success. You don't want a whole bunch of people surfacing at the last minute, claiming the founders offered them shares and threatening to sue.

I think my New Energy Finance experience was typical in that startups can be an interesting employment option for people at any stage in their career, and when they are straight out of university they usually have the least to lose and few financial responsibilities, and startups may offer interesting professional experiences. However, they are likely to offer low salaries and low job security, with stock options as a bonus. These stock options are worth having, and worth asking for more of — but there is a very high probability that they will be worth nothing, because the company will not be one of the success stories.

## 4.2. December 2009 — Acquisition by Bloomberg

In November 2009, I got a call from Michael Liebreich in a state of some excitement. He was in the process of selling the company, and needed a few things from me, such as a more formal employment contract with a notice period, and an agreement to realise the gains on the stock options he had given me. I agreed readily, even before he promised to make it a condition of the deal that I could work from the Zurich office fulltime and try living with my boyfriend who lived in Basel. I was mainly flustered and flattered to hear that I was considered an asset that the company didn't want to lose.

In December, the deal went ahead, with Bloomberg buying New Energy Finance. I got more money than I had ever dreamed of having (I later spent it on a garden). We welcomed Bloomberg staff nervously into our scruffy offices in Holborn, a part of central London that has never been stylish, and quickly got the impression that our buyers were on a somewhat different level of polish than ourselves. (When Chris Greenwood, an experienced consultant, joined New Energy Finance without fanfare in 2007, I arrived at work one morning to find he had arrived and set himself to wash up the cups in the incredibly filthy communal sink. Chris turned out to be brilliant, unflappable even at 1 am with a presentation due at 8 am, and an excellent manager, but it was the washing up which first made a positive impression on me.)

From Michael's perspective, it was a good time to sell. Michael seemed to be enjoying being a CEO and running around being a well-regarded expert and giving great presentations (which he does still), but he also needed some money that was not tied up in the company. Also, Michael was aware that while the company had established a strong lead in research on clean energy, that lead would come under increasing pressure from other energy information companies that were seeing the transformation in renewable energy affect the traditional heart of their sector. And the company would require further investment to maintain its rapid growth. Previously, in 2007, NEF had acquired a two-man carbon price modelling team, Guy Turner and Milo Sjardin, and now it had ambitious plans to expand into power markets, natural gas and water research.

Bloomberg had its own reasons for the acquisition — not only was NEF the leader in carbon and clean energy information, but its clients were willing to pay for its modelling, forecasting and interpreting developments — something Bloomberg didn't at that time know much about. One thing that nearly derailed the deal was that the price of carbon on the European carbon markets crashed while the deal was being hammered out; the only thing that saved it was that our carbon team had consistently been predicting a crash, saying that they could not see a fundamental reason why the carbon price was as high as it had been in the first place.

So in spring 2010, we moved into the shining Bloomberg offices near Liverpool Street, London. We were at this point a horde of about 60 young people in London (150 around the world) quite accustomed to wearing jeans to work unless we had a client meeting, visitors being able to wander into the office off the street if they wanted to, and sleeping on friend's floors when we went to conferences. We'd cycle to work in the rain and drape our cycling clothes over the radiator. Right from the start, Michael had decided that NEF would be what he called an AFZ, an arsehole-free zone, which was and continues to be a major perk of working here.

We certainly had a fairly informal working culture by the standards of a large company. For example, our quarterly conservative and optimistic solar installation forecasts were known as the 'coffee' and the 'beer' scenarios. The idea was that the solar team of Francesco d'Avack, Martin Simonek and I would first consider updated historical installation data, solar project pipeline, policy, investor appetite and any other information and construct a forecast for each major solar-building country for the next 2 years. Then, as the evening drew long, we'd have a couple of beers in the office, maybe a pizza, Martin would get the Slivovitz (Eastern European plum booze) out of his desk, and we'd do it again, with more optimistic results. Bloomberg does not condone drinking in the office, so the Slivovitz tradition died. The forecasts did not get worse.

Bloomberg was different to being in a startup. The offices of Bloomberg around the world are uniformly gleaming, with a glass-and-lights aesthetic. They all have 'pantries', row upon row of gleaming coffee machines and interesting and varied food — at minimum crisps and sweets and fruit, sometimes entire fresh-cooked meals. We NEFers descended on the pantry like a swarm of locusts at first, living off lattes and apples and Marmite rice cakes for days. Eventually the novelty palls a bit for all Bloomberg employees, and only the fresh-cooked food really evokes the locust reaction now. The Bloomberg employees are generally sharply dressed and very restrained, and we adapted by smartening up a bit but also getting used to all the proper Bloombergers assuming we were programmers. There is nothing wrong with being a programmer, but their dress sense is distinctive.

Integrating two companies after an acquisition is something you hear horror stories about — mass firings, formerly happy employees finding their roles changed and reduced, the acquired company being strip-mined for the most profitable bits, bullying. This acquisition was nothing like that, although there were a few culture clashes. Bloomberg has fantastic offices, infrastructure, reputation and most importantly data; there were genuine good reasons why working together made sense. And the people in charge of the acquisition from the Bloomberg side were highly competent and made us feel welcome and valued and listened to, which is a pretty important thing when your working life is being turned upside down.

The culture clashes were largely between a successful startup with minimal bureaucracy and a general trust in raw genius and quick fixes to produce good analysis, and an 8,000-person giant with defined processes in place to capture, maintain and sell data and manage staff. We got used to everything taking longer, and to needing to involve three people and explain to them why you wanted to change some data (which took longer than 'I'm the solar boss and this is solar data', which is what I was used to at NEF) before you could do it. There were other changes in the direction of more process. One of the original NEF salespeople, someone who had been there even longer than me, quit immediately, took his stock payout and went to live on a houseboat in north London rather than integrate. Travel became particularly tedious, although theoretically more comfortable, as we were issued with AMEX cards that are only accepted at relatively expensive establishments. The process of booking travel became more complex than finding the cheapest flight and hotel, and booking it. Understandably, Bloomberg wants to know where we plan to go and stay in advance, in case they need to find us or evacuate us in an emergency — a perk I hope I never have cause to be grateful for.

We got harassment training and legal compliance training and management training, which was useful. Harassment training in particular seemed like common sense that did not need to be stated at the time, but in retrospect is obviously a very wise precaution to set explicit expectations of professional behaviour in company culture.

On the whole, having processes and HR and lawyers is something companies have to do when they grow up. Integrating with Bloomberg felt like a collision, but was really just an accelerated version of the inevitable. And there are enormous upsides to working for a large and slightly bureaucratic company: job security, nice offices, a pension plan and people not looking blank when you say who you work for at conferences.

Also I got to work from the Zurich office from July 2010, and living with Björn is working out quite well so far, so I married him in 2012 and now we live together in the countryside halfway between Basel and Zurich and breed West of England geese.

# Chapter 5

# Timeline of Relevant Milestones for Solar

This is a summary of photovoltaic progress so far. Many of the events after 2005 will be examined more closely in further chapters, but a preview may help to put the story into context.

**1839:** Nineteen-year-old French scientist Edmond Becquerel demonstrates the photovoltaic effect in a liquid-based cell.

**1876:** London-based William Grylls Adams and Richard Evans Day make a solid-state PV cell from selenium.

**1879:** Patent for electric lightbulb filed, by Thomas Edison.

**1912:** The UK completes the world's first large-scale electric grid.

**1954:** Daryl Chapin, Calvin Fuller, and Gerald Pearson develop the first silicon-based solar cell, at Bell Labs. Other photovoltaic materials had been discovered by this time, but this set a record at 4% efficiency, and was later refined to 11%.

**1958:** First use of a solar cell on a satellite, an array less than 1W in size, to power the radios on Vanguard I.

**1963:** Japanese firm Sharp starts 'mass' production of solar modules. The first 242 W array (the size of a single, rather low-efficiency module today) is installed on a Japanese lighthouse.

**1964:** NASA's Nimbus I spacecraft was launched, using solar panels to power scientific instruments. It was launched on August 28 and operated successfully until September 22, when the solar panels became locked in position and failed to generate enough power. Further Nimbus satellites also used PV panels, which were substantially developed as a result of the Space Race between the US and the Soviet Union during the 1960s and 1970s.

**1970s:** The price of solar panels falls below $100/W (with work from Dr. Elliot Berman at the Exxon Corporation, no longer a company particularly well known for its constructive interest in solar research!). Solar panels for offgrid and emergency power become relatively common-place. The Cherry Hill Conference, held in 1973 in New Jersey, set a US government-funded research target of 50 cents/W for solar module cost in 1985.

**1982:** First megawatt-scale photovoltaic system built in Hesperia, California by ARCO Solar (Figure 5.1). By 1984, this has been expanded to about 6 MW, some of it using concentrated photovoltaics. During the 1990s, the plant was dismantled due to encapsulation issues with some of the panels, and because the panels were then worth more on the market than the power sold by the plant was.

**1985:** First 13.8 MW Solar Electricity Generating Systems (SEGS) plant commissioned near Kramer Junction, California. This uses parabolic trough solar thermal, not photovoltaic, technology. The SEGS complex was built up to 354 MW by 1991, by Israeli tech pioneer Luz. Unfortunately, the price of power to these plants was set as a function of the avoided cost of generating power from natural gas in California. This fell, and Luz went bankrupt in 1991 after investing $1.25 billion in the plants. The SEGS complex is still operating in 2018 — under several rounds of new ownership, and topping up solar with a significant amount

Figure 5.1.　The ARCO Solar project in Hesperia, California.
*Source*: Shutterstock.

of natural gas, but overall a technical success. Photovoltaic modules cost
$6.50/W ($12.30 in 2017 dollars, adjusted for inflation).

**1994:** Cumulative PV installation exceeds 200 MW.

**1999:** Cumulative PV installation exceeds 1 GW.

**2004:** After several smaller experiments, Germany agrees to pay a fixed
'feed-in tariff' of at least 457 euros/MWh for PV electricity, with no limits
to how much can be built. German market accelerates, firms like
SolarWorld and Conergy start up to develop projects and make modules
in Germany.

Michael Liebreich and Bozkurt Aydinoglu found New Energy
Finance, with the help of interns including this author, and a Polish
programmer called Jacek, whom Michael found on Rent-a-Coder (now
Freelance.com).

**2005:** SolarWorld, SunPower, Energy Conversion Devices, Q-Cells and Suntech all complete Initial Public Offerings (IPOs) on stock markets, raising new money and becoming stock market listed companies. Their stock prices rise.

The author starts working for New Energy Finance full time.

**2006:** Further solar IPOs including silicon makers REC and Wacker–Chemie. Annual PV installation was about 1.5 GW, limited by supply of silicon.

New Energy Finance raises first of several rounds of external funding. We move offices to a former chocolate factory near Westbourne Park tube station, and get an office kettle; great is the rejoicing.

**2007:** Spain passes law RD 661/2007 to support solar power, which does not seem important at the time but sets a very generous feed-in tariff and brings investors to the market. Spanish PV hits 85% of its target PV capacity (371 MW) by September 2007, triggering a 'grace period' of 12 months where all new projects will also be paid the feed-in tariff. Various other companies IPO. Module price still around $4/W, but global new installation hits 2.8 GW in this year.

**2008:** The end of September is the deadline for Spanish projects under RD 661/2007. In the summer, modules are not available for love or money; there are reports of cardboard modules being installed in September to fool casual inspection until real ones can be obtained. In October, module prices start to crash. Spain had installed more than 3,400 MW of its 2010 target of 400 MW.

**2009:** Module prices fall from $4/W to $2/W. The Czech Republic, which implemented a feed-in tariff in 2008, takes off as a solar market and hits 428 MW of new build PV in the year. Germany grows unexpectedly to 3.8 GW of new build. India sets target of 20 GW of solar by 2022.

New Energy Finance is acquired by Bloomberg in December, on day two of the Copenhagen Climate Summit, which spectacularly failed to deliver on all its hype.

**2010:** UK implements feed-in tariffs. Germany goes wild and installs 7 GW. World installs 18 GW. India holds world's first major solar auction, awarding bids at average price of $230/MWh. Spanish government decides not to pay the amount previously agreed for RD 661/2007 projects (a 'retroactive cut').

New Energy Finance integrates with Bloomberg.

**2011:** Module prices approach $1/W. Italy takes a turn at unexpectedly high build, with nearly 7.8 GW (Italy's National Renewable Energy Action Plan called for a total 5.6 GW by 2015). China begins to worry about solar demand, implements incentives. New PV build 28.5 GW.

**2012:** World installs 29.4 GW of PV in this year. Q-Cells goes bankrupt (later bought out by Hanwha Corp), as does Energy Conversion Devices (not bought out).

**2013:** World installs 41.6 GW — of which 14.0 GW are in China. Suntech goes bankrupt (later bought by Shunfeng).

**2014:** New Indian Prime Minister Narendra Modi sets new 2022 solar target, of 100 GW (up from 20 GW). World build 45 GW.

**2015:** World installs 56 GW of PV. Solar auction in Dubai is won at $58.4/MWh, a record low price.

**2016:** World installs about 75 GW of PV. China becomes the world's first country to have a 30 GW+ year for solar build. Solar auctions in Mexico, Dubai, Abu Dhabi and Chile won at prices below $35/MWh. Some countries delay renewable energy auctions because they do not need further power.

**2017:** World installs 98 GW of PV, of which 53 GW is in China. Module prices below $0.35/W are normal. Spain, Austria and Germany have taxes on rooftop owners self-consuming their own power (Figure 5.2).

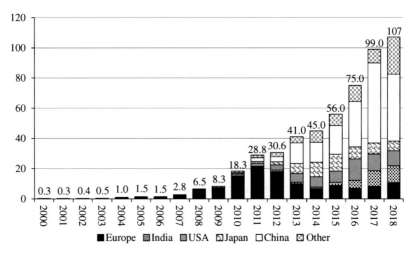

Figure 5.2.    New build PV by year, in GW.

**2018:** In the spring, China pulls back on incentive policy, causing a short-term return to oversupply and a collapse in prices. In the first half of the year, five US states (Massachusetts, California, Nevada, Hawaii and Vermont) get more than 10% of their in-state generation from solar [Hankey *et al.*, 2018]. In May, California passes bill mandating rooftop solar on most new build homes by 2020, by far the most significant rooftop mandate in the world to date. In September, California — the world's fifth largest economy — passed a bill targeting 100% zero-carbon electricity by 2045.

BNEF projects that photovoltaics will supply about 23.6% of global electricity by 2050, from about 1.8% in 2017 [Chase *et al.*, 2018]. Very few people laugh at this forecast, which includes a large amount of battery backup to sculpt power available from the grid to match demand.

# Chapter 6

# 2005–2008: The First Big Solar, Supply Constraints

I have chosen 2005 as the first year to write about mainly because it was the year I started working full time in clean energy, but it is not unreasonable: new photovoltaic installations globally rose from 1106 MW in 2004 to 1488 MW in 2005, when the German 'feed-in tariff' introduced in 2004 started to kick in. This was a landmark piece of legislation that had both intended and unintended consequences, and has been both emulated and cursed. It will be a brave government that passes an uncapped feed-in tariff for solar into law again, for reasons that will become clear. However, it was a major factor in driving the dramatic cost reductions in solar, and everyone now working in the solar industry owes the German electricity consumer a debt for paying the first mover prices.

The phrase 'feed-in tariff' is a clumsy term, translated directly from the German word Einspeisevergütung (it doesn't sound better in German. Nothing does). It refers to a guaranteed payment for every kilowatt-hour of energy generated when it is 'fed in' to the grid for the first 20 years of a plant's life. It was one of the first incentive schemes to reward actual generation, rather than making a single payment for setting up a solar installation. And, critically, there was no cap and very little paperwork; anyone building a solar plant would get the feed-in tariff, which was about three times the average power price to consumers at the time.

This feed-in tariff is paid to the project at the same rate for the next 20 years, regardless of what happens to the support level for future plants.

This is necessary because nearly all the investment in a solar plant is upfront, but it does commit the country to an ongoing liability. In Germany, this is funded through a surcharge on power bills, which as of 2017 is ~6 euro-cents/kWh for households, of the total 30 euro-cents/kWh paid for electricity. Whether you think this is a lot depends on your perspective — it certainly helps to encourage energy efficiency in German households, and is not notably unpopular with the German public.

Setting the level of an incentive is never easy for governments. The traditional method is to go and talk to the local industry and ask them how much money they would need to do something. Astonishingly, the answer usually turns out to be 'a lot'. This is partly due a genuine lack of under-standing of how efficient they could be if the volumes they were building were 10, 20, 100 times larger; I have sat in many meetings down the years with solar executives telling me that the costs achieved in Germany, Spain and the UK are completely impossible in Italy, Australia, Japan and the US. However, part is obviously pure self-interest.

In solar, this tendency for local industry to exaggerate costs used to set tariffs is exacerbated by genuine sharp reductions in cost, driven by the falling prices of solar modules and the rapid cost reductions possible when a local installation industry doing 10–20 houses/year goes to 1,000. Germany's feed-in tariff, implemented in 2004, was a raging success in that the market climbed steeply.

This feed-in tariff, available to anyone with a plot of land and solar modules, stimulated an unprecedented response from the financial markets. There had been one or two solar companies listed on stock markets before, but now investors were hungry for opportunities, and the companies were hungry for money to invest in setting up new projects and factories. Venture capital investors which had patiently waited many years found themselves able to sell their companies at a profit. (Meanwhile, I was groping my way through the unfamiliar terminology, with Michael Liebreich bellowing at me to understand why IPOs were important. It was obvious to him that these deals showed that he had picked the right time to found a company providing financial information about clean energy, because suddenly there was major interest from investors in paying to receive this information.)

For example, German solar company Conergy filed for IPO on the Frankfurt stock exchange in February 2005, selling 243 million euros' worth of shares to investors eager to participate in or increase their stake in the boom. Conergy received 104 million euros of new capital after considering shares sold by venture capital investors, and reinvested this money in developing more land and more business. It generally did not own the projects itself, instead selling them to long term investors eager to own assets with low risk (the sun is pretty reliable over a year) and reasonable reward. The investors in Conergy itself were taking a higher risk, putting their money into a company which would spend it on hiring and training staff, setting up offices, filing land use permits and other activities which might or might not bring a profit. Conergy's investors expected higher returns in exchange for the risk than the investors in solar projects themselves. The company made many investments in small solar water heating installation and distribution companies, and energy efficiency firms, built a German factory in 2006, and eventually overreached itself and went bankrupt in July 2013.

The price of solar modules had fallen continuously since 1975, when the first modules became commercially available. At that time they cost about $75/W in 2015 dollars (i.e. adjusting for inflation — they actually cost $25 in 1975, but a dollar bought a lot more back then). In 2004, the price of modules was about $4/W and continuing to fall — until Germany started buying. The price stabilised in 2004 and rose slightly to $4.20 in 2008.

The reason for the increase in price was a huge change in supply and demand. Germany was sucking up the modules on the market with an almost insatiable appetite, and Spain introduced a similar incentive in 2007 (RD 661/2007). Companies like Suntech, SolarWorld, Trina and Yingli responded by building new factories to make solar modules (and the cells and wafers that are part of the process). They quickly found themselves competing for the raw material, silicon (normally called polycrystalline silicon or polysilicon, which is just the purified silicon in chunks or rods ready to be melted and crystallised as required).

## 6.1. What Price Polysilicon?

In 2006, my colleague Lia Choi, who had joined me in specialising on solar, and I had a problem. Our clients were asking the price of the raw material polysilicon, and Michael said we had to give them an answer.

We didn't have a clue. We searched the internet for 'price of polysilicon'. We called up the press departments of polysilicon manufacturers, who told us it was a commercial secret. We combed through the financial reports of silicon manufacturers. We were stuck. Michael was insistent. For every serious commodity, he said, someone gathered the data and you could just look up the price; silicon was going to be a serious commodity, and he wanted us to be the authority on its price. He wouldn't take no for an answer.

Silicon is the fourth most common element in the earth's crust, and silicon dioxide is simply sand. The polysilicon shortage had nothing to do with silicon itself being rare. The problem is that it is difficult to purify to the level required by solar and semiconductors.

The first step is relatively easy; you take a high purity quartz sand, and heat it up with a clean type of charcoal or coke. The carbon steals the oxygen from the silicon (i.e. reduces the silicon, in chemistry terminology) and the result is about 98% pure silicon, with impurities of carbon, boron, phosphorus and other materials. Boron and phosphorus are particularly problematic as they are used later to 'dope' — change the electrical properties of — the wafer. This 98% pure silicon is known as 'metallurgical grade silicon'.

The next step is to heat the metallurgical grade silicon with acid and turn it into a gas called silane. (This is a simplification — there are several types of silane.) The gas is then put into a hot reactor vessel, with some cooler 'seeds' of silicon crystal, and condenses to form pure rods of silicon, which are broken into chunks for processing into wafers (Figure 6.1). The whole process is called the Siemens process, and is still the main way to make silicon (another process called 'fluidised bed reactor', where the silicon seeds are dropped through the gas in the reactor vessel and extracted continually from the bottom, is otherwise very similar). It is inevitably energy-intensive as different parts of the reactor vessel are being heated and cooled at the same time.

This sounds much simpler than it is. In 2004, there were only six companies (Wacker, Hemlock, REC Silicon, MEMC Electronic Materials, Tokuyama and Mitsubishi Materials) making significant volumes, and they all had teams of engineers who had been working on the problem for decades and knew how to sweet-talk a Siemens reactor into producing

Figure 6.1.   Chunks of raw polysilicon, and the finished solar cells.
*Source*: Shutterstock.

good quality silicon. However, a polysilicon factory is expensive to set up (around a billion dollars for a 10,000 tonne/year plant) and the long term average price of polysilicon up to 2004 (several years before we were trying to determine the price) had been around $25/kg, nowhere near enough to justify a large investment in a new factory. The semiconductor companies bought polysilicon under long-term contracts and had not asked for an increase in production, while the solar manufacturers took the scrap and offcuts and represented less than 10% of world demand for silicon. As solar demand soared, this waste material was no longer sufficient, and the price — in small, private negotiations — went wild.

So, back in 2006, nobody would tell us the price of polysilicon. Nobody wanted to get into trouble with their boss for either disclosing trade secrets or giving a number that might weaken the company's negotiating position with its clients or suppliers. The most talkative people were the small traders, who mostly don't have bosses, but they also had an incentive to lie, because if we published a high number the market might pay more for their inventory. A minor breakthrough was when the press officer at one of the big producers, Wacker–Chemie, took pity on me and explained (I don't think it was a secret, but it was not an angle I had thought of) that the revenue they reported for a chemicals division was 'nearly all for polysilicon this year because it was a very warm winter and hardly any salt was used on the road'. Since Wacker–Chemie had also disclosed a production figure for the chemicals division which only sold polysilicon and road salt, we had at last an approximate average price for one company (about $80/kg) and a basis for some kind of comparison.

Encouraged, we went back to anyone who would talk to us with this number and asked them if it sounded about right to them. People are a lot more talkative if you have a starting point; it is human nature to correct bad information more readily than to provide new information. Lia also determinedly turned her considerable charm on Japanese, Korean and German polysilicon people at numerous conferences, eventually convincing them we were serious (or at least persistent) and deserved answers. From this, we developed a system of anonymously asking buyers and sellers for the prices they were currently seeing on the spot market, and anonymising the results into a very official-sounding Silicon Price Index. This was surprisingly helpful to the companies, particularly the buyers, as they at least had a starting point in their negotiations with sellers. Sometimes you can look really clever just by asking people the same question at regular intervals, writing down the answers and averaging them. Michael was right.

From 2005, the solar manufacturers wanted more than the scrap silicon on the market — they needed real volumes, which meant new factories. Solar companies started asking about long-term contracts at lower prices. The polysilicon companies are by nature cautious and risk-averse (desirable characteristics for handling toxic chemicals). They had burned their fingers in the past building factories for expected demand that did not materialise, leaving expensive equipment sitting idle. They were therefore slow to respond to new demand from the slightly flaky-seeming solar sector, and insisted on large down payments and 10-year contracts to buy the polysilicon at fixed prices from solar companies.

From 2005 to 2008, solar manufacturers went to the stock markets, seeking investment to make down payments (deposits) on long-term polysilicon contracts so that polysilicon manufacturers would build factories. Spain introduced solar subsidies too, and the solar modules were flying off the shelves as fast as they could be manufactured. These down payments could be around 30% of the entire lifetime value of the polysilicon contract — an enormous financial commitment, but if the companies making solar products did not sign up, they risked being unable to manufacture anything without raw material. The stock price of a polysilicon *buyer* rose when it signed a 10-year contract, terms shrouded in secrecy, on 'take or pay' terms — i.e. even if they did not need the polysilicon in future, they had to pay for it.

The spot price of polysilicon rose to over $400/kg in 2008. Understandably, dozens of companies which had never before made polysilicon decided that this was an exciting opportunity. Firms like GT Advanced Materials sold 'turnkey manufacturing plants' ('turnkey' means that in theory the buyer gets them ready to use, they just need to turn the key to get started. Spellcheck sometimes helpfully changes this to 'turkey' in reports) to the wannabe polysilicon manufacturers. These included chemical producers and mining companies, logically enough, but also telecoms, textile and animal food production companies.

It turned out to be much tougher than expected, and nearly all these new manufacturers missed their first expected production date, and their second. Some of them poached polysilicon engineers from the Big Six (although polysilicon engineers are also cautious and tend not to jump from a well-built ship to one under construction, and certain US manufacturers reportedly threatened engineers with lawsuits should they depart to work for a rival). These firms also took down payments from customers to build their plants.

Between 2007 and 2010 we developed a 'Silicon Forward Price Index' to complement the Spot Price Index, for which we collected strictly confidential information on pricing for future sales under the contracts. This was finally possible because we had gained a reputation of being respectable silicon price analysts, and companies wanted an idea of the average price including prices from their competitors as well. The contracts were being signed at prices of $60–90/kg, sometimes at this level for 10 years in the future (remember, the price of polysilicon before the solar boom was $25/kg). The polysilicon manufacturers had the solar wafer, cell and module makers over a barrel, and investors were willing to make the massive down payments. Our Index may have stopped a few contracts being signed at even higher prices as greedy polysilicon manufacturers claimed that the current $400/kg was the new normal.

Most of the companies attempting to get into polysilicon production were in China, but at least two — French SilPro and US-based Hoku Scientific — were high-profile Western companies which burned through hundreds of millions of dollars of investor money. Ultimately, the vast majority (including SilPro and Hoku) failed, shut down and filed for bankruptcy without manufacturing any polysilicon. The down payments made by their customers were spent, and there was no way to recover the money.

Making polysilicon may be quite easy in theory, but in practice it requires several different types of chemicals expertise. It has taken some years for new entrants (including Chinese companies GCL-Poly, DAQO and TBEA) to get good at it. As of 2018, however, the polysilicon price squeeze is over and at least a dozen companies are good at manufacturing the stuff to solar standards.

# Chapter 7

# The Magic of the Experience Curve

One of the problems with economics and finance as sciences is that they tend to find a relationship in the past and assume it will continue into the future. This works well, until it doesn't. Unlike with physics, there tend to be more variables than actual data, and experiments (for example, policy changes in the real world) generally change all the variables at once in a very unscientific way. It's very difficult to tell what will happen until it does, after which it is so obvious that any idiot should have predicted it.

One example of this is with the photovoltaic module experience curve. This is sometimes called the Swanson Effect after Dr Richard Swanson of SunPower. Although Dr Swanson has contributed greatly to the research driving the experience curve, he is the first to say that he did not invent it. If anything, it should be called the Maycock Effect after Paul Maycock, a market researcher who collected the most comprehensive set of solar module pricing data from 1975 to 2003, and whose data forms the basis of most attempts to construct this curve, including ours.

Experience curves are found in many industries, and are an empirical relationship between the amount of experience the human species has at doing something, and how cheaply we can do it. (An empirical relationship is one which appears to hold in practice, but cannot be mathematically proven.) In the production of many commodities, the cost per unit decreases by a fixed amount (the 'learning rate') for every doubling of cumulative experience. This produces a curve declining exponentially to an asymptote, or a straight line in a log–log chart (see Figure 7.1).

45

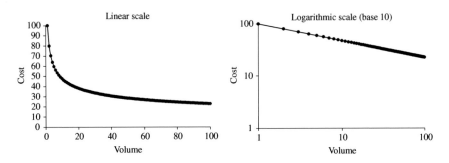

Figure 7.1.    A generic experience curve.

The shape makes intuitive sense — when something is very new, it is easy to find ways to make it more cheaply, while even a small improvement in a well-established manufacturing process is difficult to achieve because all the easy tweaks have been done already. It is interlinked with economies of scale, and does not take into account raw material prices and other factors. For example, drilling oil wells in the sea probably follows an experience curve, but over time the near-shore oilfields have been explored and exhausted, so future wells will need to be further offshore in deeper water and may therefore be more expensive. This is also a factor in offshore wind farm costs for the same reason — some offshore wind farms are just onshore wind farms in a puddle, some are in the deep sea.

The classic exponential curve shape usually means that cost reductions get slower over time, because it normally takes longer and longer to double cumulative manufactured capacity. It isn't a perfect relationship, but it's not a bad way of describing the behaviour of prices for manufactured commodities. Moore's Law, which is a special case of this, describing the pricing per unit of computing power with underlying assumptions about deployment growth rates. Formulated in 1965, Moore's Law states that the number of components (transistors) of an integrated circuit doubles about every 2 years. Part of the reason that this law holds is that the computing industry uses it as a target, but it is also just a function of increasing scale with a high growth rate, and the experience curve.

Photovoltaic module manufacturing is a clear example of an experience curve, and since 1975, modules have become 24–29% (depending on exactly where you think the line of best fit falls — as of 2018 we incline towards 28%) cheaper on a per W basis for every doubling of cumulative capacity.

This has not been simple, linear progress when viewed from the inside. Professor Martin Green of the University of New South Wales, Director of the Australian Centre for Advanced Photovoltaics, remembers a famous 1973 working group in Cherry Hill, New Jersey which established guidelines and targets for US government-funded solar research. "They were thinking of the mid-1980s as a target date for solar panels at 50 cents a Watt [about a dollar per W in 2017 dollars]" he says.

This Cherry Hill target was wildly missed, as Figure 7.2 shows. The price of solar panels in 1985 was $6.50/W, or about $12.30/W in 2017 dollars. However, Green says, the research resulting from the 1973 working group established a lot of the fundamentals of solar technology today, such as screen printing of solar cells, and lamination of solar cells under glass (silicone rubber was previously used as an encapsulant until the 1980s, but it was not fully hail-resistant and Australian parakeets liked to eat it). "The commercial industry was not vibrant during the 1980s" he said in an interview for this book in July 2018. "A lot of the firms were oil

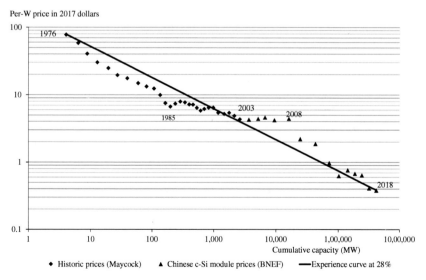

Figure 7.2. The BloombergNEF crystalline silicon photovoltaic module experience curve, early 2019.

companies doing greenwashing, and just trying not to lose too much money from solar. They weren't looking for new technology in the same way they are today. For example, we developed a buried-contact cell [which offered better efficiency] but one of the firms did not want to adopt it because they'd have to update all their data sheets [the official product description] if they increased their cell efficiency".

The experience curve is driven by improvements in efficiency, better conductive pastes, bigger individual cells, less silicon wastage in slicing, thinner silicon wafers, better structural design of cells, and optimisation of anti-reflective coatings and encapsulants. It continues the relentless grind to lower costs to this day (more details in Chapter 18).

There are a couple of common fallacies in the experience curve analysis. One is that the learning rate can change over time. If it does this, then it's not an experience curve (and most likely you are looking at temporary fluctuations in the demand or supply situation, or a move to a completely different technology). The other is to apply them to things that are not manufactured commodities. Experience curves generally work only for manufactured commodities, so it is difficult if not impossible to calculate them from local data, including non-manufactured cost factors like installation. In practice, what level to disaggregate the experience curve to is a matter of considerable discussion; in solar modules, a tweak that increases cost at the wafer level may ultimately decrease cost at the module level, so trying to separate wafer and module experience curves would not be helpful. My feeling is that only the module experience curve, and perhaps the inverter experience curve, make sense as a calculation.

The ~20% learning rate for solar modules was well established in academic literature from 1975 to 2003 [De La Tour *et al.*, 2013], although academic literature went rather silent in 2004 as the price rose slightly and then stayed flat. A few commentators called it the death of the experience curve, and suggested that the cost of solar panels had hit a fundamental lower limit.

Essentially, they were confusing the price and cost of solar panels. Prices had declined broadly in line with costs until 2004, when demand suddenly surged because of generous German feed-in tariffs. This demand overwhelmed supply, which was limited by the amount of available polysilicon. Pricing stayed approximately flat from 2004 through to 2008, despite several doublings of cumulative global capacity to drive costs down — in essence the market was pricing solar panels at exactly the level required to absorb the feed-in tariff, rather than following costs down. Costs, meanwhile were not following the experience curve because — as we knew from our Silicon Price Index — the price of silicon had increased by a factor of 10. But there was no reason to think that it would stay that high once more silicon became available.

In May 2007, sitting in the back row of the Renewable Energy Finance Forum, the major conference for clean energy investors in New York at the time, Michael Liebreich sketched out what he thought was going to happen next. As soon as silicon supply could match demand, the price of solar cells and panels would collapse back to where the cost experience curve said it should be at that point. There would be a blood-bath among producers and a bonanza for installers. Later in the event, he presented this on stage based on illustrative figures he had made up, and was greeted with a wall of scepticism. At the time, most investors and companies were making 10-year business plans around projected prices of $3–4/W, with prices gently sloping down from where they had been stuck between 2004 and 2008. Michael was convinced they were in for a shock.

As soon as he was off the stage, he emailed to tell me what he had done. We urgently needed our own experience curve to give Michael's illustrative numbers some credibility. My colleague Lia Choi and I ran the numbers and produced a short report predicting a 40% fall in module prices when polysilicon demand and supply came back into balance. As the author I have to admit that it wasn't a very good report compared with our later efforts, using a poor proxy for module cost, too short a history, and a rather arbitrary means of predicting when the shortage of polysilicon would end (early 2009). Nevertheless it was basically correct in stating that when undersupply ended, the price of solar modules would fall not 10% or 20%, but a lot (it wasn't wrong about the timing, either).

In hindsight, it is amazing how many people missed the fact that the pricing was unsustainable — according to our Silicon Price Index, the spot price of polysilicon was over $400/kg, which meant that some Chinese and Taiwanese companies were paying that rate and still making a slim profit on modules selling around $4.20/W. But a solar module required roughly 8 g of polysilicon per W, which costs about \$3.20 at this price (as of 2017, average polysilicon use is down to about 5 g a W — the experience curve is a wonderful thing). The Chinese and Taiwanese firms were clearly able to do all the manufacturing from wafers to modules for less than \$1/W. Meanwhile, more established companies in Europe and the US (Evergreen Solar, Q-Cells, Schott) had locked in contracts around the \$100/kg mark (about 80 US cents per W) and were still not making a great profit selling at \$4.20/W. It should have been clear that if the Chinese and Taiwanese manufacturers got hold of cheaper polysilicon, they would be the winners of any pricing war, and the prices would be much lower than anyone else was predicting. This was also inevitable — even if more polysilicon did not become available on the spot market, giant Chinese firms like Suntech, Yingli Solar and Trina Solar were playing the game of raising money on the public markets to lock in long-term contracts.

Solar companies had been planning for a future of limitless expansion and mild decreases in price, limited only by their technical ability to deliver. We knew they were in for a shock, and so it proved, for the experience curve had continued to work in the background even as the polysilicon shortage prevented prices from falling.

# Chapter 8

# September 29, 2008: When the Solar Boom Went Bust

In 2007, the Spanish government made an amendment to a law, subsidising big solar projects in Spain for the first time. This was one of the most regretted pieces of legislation ever passed in solar. The Spanish government appears to have copied the German law, and asked solar companies what level of incentive they would like.

As in Germany, the government put no restrictions on how many plants could get the tariffs — except that once a certain level of installation was reached, there would be a 1-year 'grace period' during which projects could be finished and still received the tariff. This was based on the assumption that solar projects would take 6–8 months to build, and allowing a few months for projects which were already in the planning process when the grace period started. In photovoltaics, the level to trigger the grace period was 371 MW, and was expected to be hit sometime in 2010.

Belén Gallego, an entrepreneur who was running solar technology and development conferences in Spain at the time, says "Everyone knew that it was not a wise decision by the government to not limit the amount of MW, we knew it was going to get very large very quickly. There was a gold rush mentality, but we did not know how bad it was going to get."

Another feature of the Spanish law was that it paid a much higher tariff to projects smaller than 100 kW than to projects over 100 kW — but did not specify how a project under 100 kW was defined. Spot the loophole?

Developers filed applications for tens or hundreds of 100 kW sites right next door to one another, meaning that they could get all the economies of scale of building a big project without losing the higher rate tariff. The tariff was therefore much more generous than originally anticipated, and very popular. By September 2007, the capacity cap set in May 2007 for photovoltaics had been exceeded and the 1-year 'grace period' had begun.

It turns out that you don't need 6–8 months to build a 100 kW photovoltaic plant. 6–8 weeks is more accurate, if you have the paperwork in place. The main constraint on the Spanish solar market between September 2007 and September 2008 was the availability of solar modules — which was still limited by the shortage of polysilicon. It was not just a game for large companies, either, and in fact small family firms often proved more nimble at securing permits, negotiating engineering contracts and securing short-term finance to build.

The deadline for the end of the grace period was September 28, 2008, and as it approached, a frantic hurry swept the Spanish market. Modules were difficult to source at any price, and there are stories of project buyers putting up fake cardboard modules in order to pretend to casual observers that the deadline had been met, planning to replace them with real modules after the deadline. There was no way the government could manage a thorough inspection in a timely manner, and 350 projects lost their subsidies in 2010 when inspection finally caught up with them and established that they could not have had the generating equipment in place as claimed (there are unsubstantiated reports of diesel generators being used to power unfinished solar plants, with the owners seeing no reason to turn them off at night). "People were working weekends to get the plants built" says Belén Gallego. "But I think most of the rush was in the planning and negotiating stages in the few months before the deadline. I remember a lot of haste and nervousness, new companies formed every day offering solar services as it wasn't difficult for them to get work. One thing that wasn't obvious to people was that the regional governments and local politicians of Spain were competing to push technology in their regions, trying to attract business and jobs to their part of Spain. There was a lot of optimism from governments even though a lot of people knew it was unsustainable." The support of local governments helped developers and accelerated the growth of the market.

In total, about 3,400 MW of photovoltaic projects were built in Spain in 2007 and 2008 — compared with the 436 MW targeted by 2010. This sounds great if you are a solar advocate, but it left the bill with the Spanish electricity generation sector, which was already regulated into unprofitability and kept afloat by direct government handouts. This was a known problem, and the government was intending to reform the regulation as soon as they'd figured out how, but the solar boom made it much more acute.

The other effect was that as the sun rose on September 29, 2008, global demand for solar modules was significantly lower than it had been the previous week. Manufacturing industry leader Q-Cells issued a profit warning, "due to short notice unexpected developments… the uncertainty and the weakening market demand arising from the financial crisis have resulted in a number of Q-Cells' customers postponing agreed deliveries until next year. These volumes could not be placed elsewhere at short notice" — which seems a little surprising, since the end of the Spanish boom was hardly short notice. Q-Cells' Chinese competitors Suntech and JA Solar cut their guidance (the forecasts they had shared with the stock market) for sales in the fourth quarter. Prices immediately started to plummet from $4.20/W in Q3 2008, to the surprise of many analysts, who had expected that Germany would absorb the extra modules and that the fall of the Spanish market would cause only a 10% or so drop in module price. I'm proud to look back at a report we published at the end of 2008 [Bullard *et al.*, 2008] and see that we predicted $2.40/W ("perhaps lower") as a module price for 2009, based on an estimate of margins being made across the value chain. Actual module prices fell to $2/W in the year.

In one way, though, the other analysts had a point — Germany's solar market did have a bumper time in late 2008, installing 1.9 GW and cushioning the fall a little. German solar projects got a lot more profitable with the newly cheap modules. However, the situation was about to get a lot tougher for the manufacturers and for some of the investors.

To cut a long story short, the Spanish solar companies which had built projects in such a hurry did not get to keep much of their gains.

On December 23, 2010, the Spanish government introduced a new decree which essentially said it would pay the agreed subsidies only for part of each solar plant's output. At a stroke this decree cut revenues from the plants by between 7% and 30%, and further changes have been imposed over the years since. Some developers had done well out of the market by selling projects to other investors at a high price before this happened.

Spanish banks, especially small ones, were affected by the retroactive cuts because they had lent money to projects now unable to pay it back. Some owners defaulted on the payments, meaning that the bank now owns the projects — something the banks did not really want to do as they had no real interest in running portfolios of small projects. In some cases, they had even lost track of the projects. Belén Gallego says, "The small banks were bundled up in larger banks during the financial crisis. You cannot imagine the amount of stranded assets that resulted. When I was working as a technical advisor [in 2016–2017] we would get one of the big banks coming to us and saying 'we have located 50 more projects that we have in our assets, from 20 different local banks we acquired, and we don't know where they are.' Literally 8 years later this bank was trying to figure out what they have on their books. We found ourselves doing all the work to figure out who owned these plants, if they were abandoned, who was doing the maintenance."

Unfortunately, 'retroactive tariff changes' (cuts to incentives agreed for existing projects) became a brief trend across Europe from 2009 to 2014, with Bulgaria, the Czech Republic and Romania backpedalling on their promised generosity. Although many investors lost money, this had surprisingly little effect on the solar industry as a whole outside Southern and Eastern Europe.

The moral of the whole sad story is that if something seems too good to be true, it probably is, especially when it is a badly designed solar subsidy. However, as of early 2018, Spain has reformed its electricity sector and started to reduce the deficit, and project developers are starting to trust the market again.

# Chapter 9

# Forecasting Methods: Difficulties and Discontinuities

Physicist Niels Bohr is reported to have said "Prediction is difficult, especially about the future". While significant strides have been made in weather forecasting and predicting at least the frequency of earthquakes over the past 100 years, predictions relating to human behaviour and economics remain direly inaccurate. As statistician Nate Silver says in his excellent book *The Signal and the Noise* (2012), "we are unable to predict recessions more than a few months in advance, and not for want of trying". He observes that in December 2007, economists on The Wall Street Journal forecasting panel predicted only a 38% likelihood of recession in the next year, which was remarkable because the data would later show that the economy was already in recession at the time.

Energy experts and organisations have an equally poor record on forecasting oil price, electricity demand, power price, the uptake of solar panels, or pretty much anything. Experts miss black swans, under- or overestimate trends, ignore data that would challenge their preconceived notions, and make other errors or misjudgements. They have their own biases, either explicit (oil companies are unlikely to forecast very low oil prices when the rest of the market disagrees) or implicit. A true expert gathers a wealth of information and weighs it mentally and, often, uses a model to understand what it implies.

Unfortunately, sometimes the more information you have, the more interpretations it can support — and Nate Silver writes extensively about the tendency of human forecasters to cherry-pick whatever data supports the forecaster's preconceptions, and sometimes to miss obvious conclusions in a wealth of irrelevant detail.

Even the closest companies to the data do not always get the results right, and may have deeply ingrained biases. Figure 9.1 details how the Australian Electricity Market Operator (AEMO), despite presumably having the best available data on Australian electricity demand, has consistently forecast that electricity demand will rise — while in fact, due to recession and energy efficiency improvements, it has fallen. The forecast does seem to be getting better from 2014, though, due to a combination of a slight uptick in electricity demand and also to AEMO adapting its methodology to more recent data. For example, AEMO began to account for the contribution of rooftop photovoltaics, which it perceives as a reduction of electricity demand to the grid.

You might legitimately ask what the point is of making forecasts at all. The main reason is that the alternative is worse; if you have not even tried to understand the future, how can you plan for it? Should you invest money and make public policy at random, or simply do nothing and hope Fate is kind? Even a bad forecast may be better than no forecast.

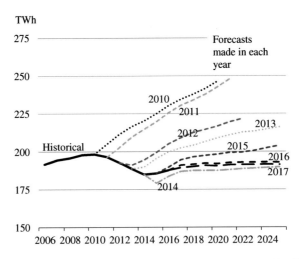

Figure 9.1.   Australian electricity demand, and forecasts by the Australian Energy Market Operator (charted by BloombergNEF).

One rather cynical reason why there is a market for forecasts, even when forecasts do not perform well, is encapsulated in the saying that "nobody ever got fired for hiring McKinsey or buying IBM" — an appeal to authority can be a way to pass the buck. In the power markets, a Finnish company called Pøyry produces the European standard for power price forecasts, and these go into a lot of investment proposals, although the BloombergNEF power team considers them to be on the high side.

A slightly less cynical rationale is that hiring an expert will give you not just the numbers but the means to help you convince potential investment partners that you know what you are talking about, much more quickly than if you had to research the topic yourself. You can ask them questions, get juicy details, learn smart lines of arguments and ideas. The information conveyed may be parallel to the question of whether the investment should be made, but being able to talk smart is an important quality in getting that investment. Also, you can pick your experts depending on how much you are convinced by their rationales.

Right or wrong, it is unlikely that anyone will remember your forecasts years later when the excrement hits the ventilation. Nonetheless, at BloombergNEF we do our best to get them right. We publish our forecasts to multiple parties, and we expect to be around next year with an updated but ideally not completely different forecast. For this reason and because we gain knowledge, we hope, we get better at it. Our old forecasts are still available to any client who wants to look, and we revisit our mistakes and try to learn from them. You can, if you wish, take a number of competitor forecasts and average them to see if you get a 'wisdom of crowds' effect (for this reason, my team tries hard not to be deflected from our house view only by a different figure coming out of a competitor. If we did that, we'd end up all publishing the same numbers for no good reason).

When data starts getting complicated, when there are feedback loops and outside parameters that influence events in complex ways, it may make sense to build a model. Models are much misunderstood by laymen and even by people who should know better; as statistician George Box is reported to have said, "all models are wrong. Some are useful". They can certainly help us understand complex behaviour and which factors are important, and good modellers come back each year to test and improve their work on the basis of the newest data.

One major weakness of models, however, is that they are only as good as the input data ('garbage in, garbage out'). The main metrics my team have been forecasting over the years — solar new installation in a year, and price of solar components — are areas where there is no final answer in terms of what the data is. So my team has spent far more time looking for good data about the past, than developing complex models for the future.

Installation in a year for an individual country may be known fairly well if the power grid operator tracks individual projects and publishes a total, as in Germany, Spain and Italy (though the grid operators here have been known to come back and restate this figure a few years later). Other countries are not so organised, and we may have to rely on estimates from industry associations, trade bodies, incentive programme monitors and local companies. We also collect total production estimates from the top 50 or so cell and module manufacturers, allowing us to triangulate on world new build in a year. Since 2015, we buy data from a Chinese customs data monitor on the value of photovoltaic goods going to individual countries and globally, which also helped us to identify countries which are major offgrid markets and refine our estimates. (It turns out that Pakistan, Iran and Yemen buy far more solar panels than we expected, probably because of poor grid access in these countries.) We have often had to revise installation numbers several years old, or make crude estimates when the official figures apply to timeframes that are not whole years. China has a particularly charming habit of announcing in January that it connected massively more capacity to the grid in the previous year than anyone imagined. The Japanese reporting year runs from April to April, not January to January. India, Thailand and the United States report AC capacity — the capacity of inverters connected — rather than, like nearly everyone else, the module capacity. (AC capacity is normally 10–50% less than DC capacity — further details in Section 18.3 of Chapter 18. I have used DC capacity throughout this book, and believe that this should be the default worldwide for photovoltaics).

In short, all historical solar new build estimates in MW have considerable uncertainty — plus or minus 5% — even years later. This is probably not unusual among economic metrics, but may come as a shock to other people with a physics or other hard science background.

This being the case, why would we expect our forecasts to be either good or useful? Well, forecasts of new build are usually mainly used for figuring out where to put offices and staff, and whether to expand or scale back operations. The MW numbers are not, fortunately, required to be precise.

The 2-year forecast that we produce is therefore a short-term snapshot based on large projects we see, supportive policies in place, contracts signed and a general sense of where things are going relative to the past. As of 2018, we cover nearly 50 markets, with local analysts sitting down at least once a quarter to consider if revision is necessary based on new data or developments. Figure 9.2 shows the progress of our forecasts over time, with Q1 2018 being the most recent — and therefore hopefully the most accurate — the thick, highest line.

We have almost always underestimated the future growth. We have apparently got a little better since 2013, probably because this was the point where we started using a high 'Rest of World' buffer in the forecast — basically, a sizeable chunk of forecast demand on top of the known markets. This is necessary because firstly there are always new markets

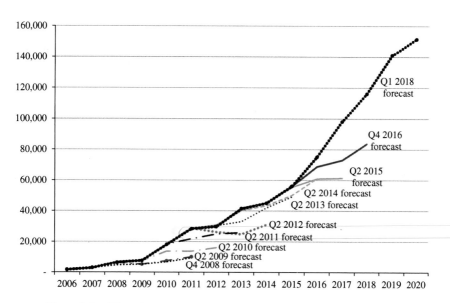

Figure 9.2. BloombergNEF forecasts of global new PV installation, MW.

that you find out about late in a year ("Trade press PV Tech says Algeria installed 268 MW in 2015, and it seems to be confirmed by government data? We didn't even have Algeria in our forecasts") and secondly, my team members more often underestimate their own markets than they overestimate them.

Underestimation is a systematic bias in renewable energy forecasting, and it occurs partly because renewable energy analysts wish to seem objective rather than being cheerleaders for their sector. This also avoids arguments with clients (which include large oil, gas and electricity companies, who are not necessarily anti-renewables but can be culturally resistant to forecasts of extreme change. Solar developers are often also resistant to high forecasts which may alert the government to an unsustainable subsidy, or attract competition). It's easier to defend a low forecast than a high one. Also, when you are an analyst or employee working in a country which installed 5 MW last year, it's hard to imagine a 500 MW market — even though solar incentives can quickly create exactly that.

Towards the end of 2010, we were perplexed by the fact that module prices were holding relatively firm even though our estimates of available manufacturing capacity significantly exceeded known demand. Major markets were Germany and Italy, both of which reported grid connection data monthly with a few months of lag time, and did not explain what was going on. Uncertain, we assigned the missing modules to Germany, predicting a 10–11 GW/year. Even in January 2011, we continued to report that Germany must have installed 10 GW — even while Germany's October and November grid connection statistics came in suggesting it was much lower. In February 2011, we got the answer to the missing module problem: Italy (which we had pegged at about 1.2 GW), had installed the missing 3.4 GW, but had not previously reported them, because they were not yet grid connected. (They had a special legal exemption and became known as the 'Salva Alcoa' projects, which means 'saving aluminium'. I have never figured out why.)

A more recent error was our 2016 new build estimate for China, which was 26–27 GW at the beginning of 2017 (notice also how much the magnitude of the numbers has changed over time! We thought 10 GW a year for a single market was almost unbelievable in 2010, and indeed,

Germany came in at about 7.2 GW — making our overall estimate for 2010 at the end of the year fairly good). We were quite happy with this Chinese estimate, because most of China's major support schemes for PV have a quota system — the federal government promises each province that it will fund a certain volume of projects at a pre-set price, and the provincial governments are supposed to allocate this quota to individual companies to build. The total quota available was limited to about 25 GW, and the programmes not subject to quota were small. So we were quite surprised when, in early January, China's National Energy Administration announced that 34.2 GW had been grid connected in 2016. It appears that some companies had been building solar projects early without guaranteed support, to get to the front of the queue when quota is allocated for 2017. Whether this is a good strategy or not, time will tell. (Also about 4 GW of projects were probably built in 2015 and grid connected in 2016.) In any case, it blew our buffer on the forecast for 2016. We saw a very similar story in 2017, although the Chinese government issues a further 86.5 GW of 'quota' in August 2017, encouraging developers to keep building.

Using the Rest of World forecast as a buffer to account for "unknown unknown" demand is intensely criticised by clients — how can you say that a substantial chunk of the world's solar module production is just going to be sold without knowing where — but it has significantly improved our forecast accuracy. On the other hand, the same could be said for any way we made forecasts higher. For this reason, the most accurate forecast of solar deployment made in 2010 for 2015 was almost certainly Greenpeace's, which foresaw 98–108 GW of cumulative PV capacity by 2015. It was actually 243 GW, and Greenpeace appear to have made it simply by extrapolating current growth rates of over 40% on new build, but it was much closer than anyone else's because it was the highest. Simply extrapolating growth rates gave a better result than all my team's knowledge and work; however, it's clearly not something that can continue forever. This is a major problem with forecasting discontinuities (points at which the future does not simply look like the past extrapolated) — figuring out where they are going to stop.

Clients frequently want to build a 'proper' model for the solar sector (incorporating 'simple' factors like policy, power prices, consumer behaviour, amount of roof space, etc.) and usually send a bright intern to use our data to crack the problem. The intern wrangles the data, fails to find consistent patterns (if you give people subsidy to install solar, they usually do — but you cannot predict how many people will, or when the subsidies will be removed...) and leaves after three months wiser and without revolutionising the world of solar power forecasting.

Since 2007, very early in the history of the company, Michael Liebreich has insisted that we have a central energy modelling team, bringing together the outputs from all the different teams into a single global power forecast. This takes inputs on electricity demand by country, the planned building and scheduled decommissioning of coal and nuclear plants, and cost of generation of various energy sources (most notably solar and wind, which are getting cheaper). The exercise is very broadly similar to what the International Energy Agency (IEA) does in Paris — but less inclined to predict more of the same, and more open to incorporating disruptive data and extrapolating observed cost trends. (The IEA has been much criticised for forecasting low renewables uptake in its World Energy Outlook scenarios, although it does have a renewables division, led since 2007 by Paolo Frankl and supported by Dr Cedric Philibert, which produces much more realistic forecasts for renewables uptake).

The modelling effort at New Energy Finance has, as with the IEA forecasts, been moving in the right direction. The current model includes energy demand changes by country (with assumptions about energy efficiency improvements), planned nuclear, coal and gas plant buildings and decommissionings, and the cost of various energy sources; when a country needs more energy supply, it builds the 2–3 cheapest options (since countries very rarely only choose one source of energy, for security reasons). It also crudely considers how well the output from solar and wind will match times of high electricity demand (generally, photovoltaics generates when power demand for air conditioning is high, although the output falls off sharply in late afternoon when the outside temperature is hottest). The BloombergNEF model's output is fairly rational, at least for solar, in that it builds a lot of solar capacity by 2050 in countries which are sunny and need more power generation.

As of 2018, the model also considers longer periods of extreme conditions, such as whole weeks of low solar and wind output and high electricity demand in a Northern European winter. This would drain the biggest battery likely to be economic, because the battery would only be used a couple of times per year. The model responds with a legitimate solution — it builds open cycle gas turbines (low-efficiency but cheap gas power plants) to supply electricity during these periods. It doesn't really matter that these power plants are inefficient, since they are cheap and only run in semi-emergencies.

The point of having this model is not to give a truly accurate output when the BloombergNEF team put in their favoured inputs (events will almost certainly not come to pass as the model says); the main point is to ensure that the forecasts produced by each BloombergNEF sectoral team have to be internally consistent — you can't have the total of all the electricity production outstrip the global demand for electricity. You can also play with the inputs and look at what happens. Models are for avoiding blunders and understanding the world, not for predicting it.

# Chapter 10

# How Markets Set Power Prices

Energy is a sector in which even the most ardent proponents of the free market admit the need for some regulation. The decisions made — what sort of power plants to build, whether to add gas pipelines, whether to invest in the power grid — will affect the country for the next 30–50 years, and conditions may change significantly. Building a fleet of gas plants at a time when gas is cheap leaves a country vulnerable to higher gas prices or disruption in supply in future. Building a coal plant today risks higher coal prices and carbon taxes in future. Solar and wind plants will not suffer from higher input costs in future, but new plants will get cheaper, and when solar or wind becomes a substantial part of electricity supply, intermittency becomes a problem. (Back in 2006, when no country had more than 2% of its electricity from solar, I thought 'what happens at night?' was a dumb question because there was no risk of running out of backup. It's not a dumb question today, although it is generally asked by people who don't actually want to discuss possible answers. It's also not become a huge problem yet, even as some places — Greece, Italy, California — edge toward 10% solar in their total electricity generation. Chapter 22 discusses this.)

Electricity provision is a natural monopoly — the bigger a firm is and the more power plants it operates, the cheaper it can sell power to consumers, and it is likely to gain market share. In theory, a completely unregulated utility could drive all other utilities out of business and then charge as much as it likes for power, which would not be in the long-term interests of a country.

Consequently most governments set up an energy regulator, a public body meant to stop utilities behaving badly. Its job is to approve or reject utility plans to build new power plants, merge, change power prices or make other significant business decisions. For example, a utility might ask to increase power prices to cover the cost of additional grid maintenance, or to build a new power plant, or just because it wasn't recovering its costs, and the regulator decides if this is reasonable. The UK regulator is Ofgem, but nearly all countries and most US states have their own.

Generally, energy regulators encourage a diversified mixture of cheap power sources, so that the country is not solely dependent on one source of energy. The regulator is quite conservative about new sources, as unlike companies they do not make any profit and from being right to approve changes, and will be blamed for anything that goes wrong. They are also responsible for making sure that utilities can cover their costs and make a reasonable profit from the revenue they get by selling power to consumers, that any subsidies get paid and that the lights stay on. In Germany, the UK and most other countries, renewable energy subsidies are paid initially by the utilities, which are allowed to collect the money back from power prices. Consumers might complain about the portion of renewable energy on the bill (in Germany, this is now roughly 20% of total electricity price for households) but at least it is transparent and there is a system for paying.

In Spain in 2008, this system had broken down, and utilities were forced by regulators to undercharge for power even before renewable energy subsidies became important. The utilities then in theory would collect the money back from the government, which by 2012 owed them 20 billion euros (according to the IEA's Spain Energy Policy review in that year) and had no plan to pay. Not surprisingly, this later turned out to be a problem.

Regulators are often involved in setting the level of subsidies, which depends on the cost of generating power from other sources and the cost of generating power from renewables.

In addition to the parts of the power system controlled directly by regulators, many countries have a 'spot power market' where companies

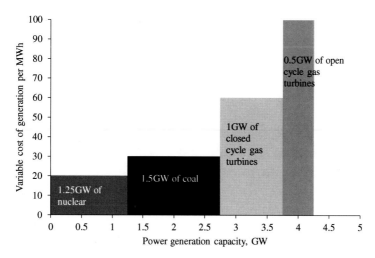

Figure 10.1.   A hypothetical dispatch curve for one period on a power market. If demand is 2 GW, the spot price of power will be $30/MWh. If demand rises to 3 GW, the price will rise to $60/MWh.

buy and sell power in small amounts every hour, or even every 15 minutes in more sophisticated markets, one day or one hour before delivery. Although most power is usually sold under long-term contracts, the spot market helps match short-term supply and demand. The price is set by the 'short-run marginal cost of generation' (SRMC — also known as variable cost of production), an important concept which merits further explanation.

Let's start by looking at a system with no renewables, because this represents the set of problems that modern power markets are structured to solve. When we introduce renewables, you will see why we encounter difficulties. Figure 10.1 represents the power plants in operation in a rather simple 4.25 GW grid, ordered from the lowest SRMC to the highest. Nuclear is the lowest in SRMC, because once you have built an expensive nuclear plant, the additional cost of generating a MWh from it in this period is very low — in fact, problems will arise for the operator if it needs to be abruptly switched off. For this reason, the nuclear plant operator bids the lowest price, enough to cover fuel and maintenance. (The debate on how much nuclear energy costs is considerably more complicated than this because the full cost of nuclear includes, at the very least, the cost to build the power plant and a return for investors, which is the majority of the cost. This will be returned to in Chapter 13.) In this scenario, if demand for power is less than 1.25 GW, the price will be $20/MWh — incredibly cheap. This is what happens in the middle of the night in France, which gets over 70% of its electricity from nuclear. (French utilities pass on this cheap nighttime power to consumers, and many use electricity to heat up their hot water tanks, effectively storing the energy for daytime use.)

If the market needs more than 1.25 GW of power, the nuclear plant is not sufficient and the buyers need to pay for coal. Coal plants are also cheap to run, but do require fuel and maintenance. They are also quite hard to turn off and on again quickly, so realistically are likely to be running most of the time.

If the demand for power is more than 2.75 GW, the closed cycle gas turbines (CCGT — the normal, high efficiency type of gas plant) will need to be switched on, and the power price will rise sharply. Most of the time, in most developed countries, the power demand will sit in this region, making CCGT plants the marginal source of power. They are also more flexible than either coal or nuclear, which means that can be turned on or off again with relative ease (though are often kept moving as 'spinning reserve' through hours of disuse so they can be brought back online quickly). It's probable that our fictional grid usually has power demand between 2.75 and 3.75 GW, allowing it to use gas turbines to some extent but not all the time, and average power prices around $60/MWh.

If power demand exceeds 3.75 GW, the closed cycle gas turbines will not be enough. This is when 'open cycle gas turbines' (OCGTs — inefficient power plants) that are cheap to build and quick to shut on and off — switch on. These are for semi-emergency power, and would not be expected to run many hours per year. A truly desperate grid, or one in an oil-rich country, might also use diesel generators as a last resort.

Hydroelectric power would fall somewhere in the middle of this; most hydro plants can be ramped up and down quickly, while some waste the power and some store it behind a dam when the plant is not required to be generating.

In theory, the prices on the spot market should be able to go from zero to any level — if power demand is high enough, open-cycle gas turbines or even diesel generators become the most economic way to generate the last MW during a certain period, or the utility could simply allow some blackouts. Another option is for the utility or regulator to literally phone round industrial energy users and offer them money to turn off their factories during periods of power supply crunch (this has been done in Texas). Part of the function of the so-called smart grid would be to automate this process and divert power from places it will not be missed in the short term. We will return to these complexities in Chapter 22.

While in theory one could let the market set the price, most governments do not want utilities to decide that the lowest cost option is to cut some customers off temporarily if it isn't economic to serve them. Governments also prefer that customers are not handed an unexpectedly huge bill because for two hours in December power demand was so high that utilities had to fire up their most inefficient diesel generator and pay an aluminium factory to shut down. This is historically not a big problem in Western economies, which have enough gas plants to cover power demand.

The problem comes when you introduce a large amount of wind or solar power into the system. Wind and solar power have no marginal cost. Figure 10.2 shows what happens when 1 GW of solar is being generated.

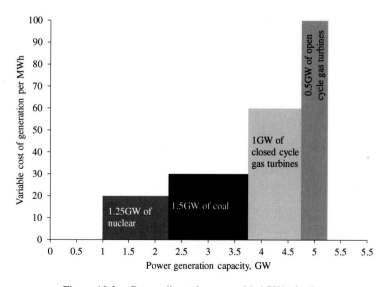

Figure 10.2.   Power dispatch curve with 1GW of solar.

The solar plants are not going to shut down just because the price of power is low. Most can use their inverter tuning mechanisms to stop generating, but why would they do that while the price of power is positive? It doesn't cost them anything to operate.

This means that while the sun shines, unless power demand is over 3.75 GW, the gas plants are not going to be turned on (and if it is very sunny when demand is low, the price of power can even drop to zero, or if the grid is legally required to take the power, negative. Negative market pricing of power now happens several times a year in Denmark and Germany, because shutting down fossil fuel plants costs money, so the market needs to pay them to shut down for a few hours and prevent overgeneration). As soon as the sun drops, the gas plants will need to be fired up.

Intrinsically, not running fossil fuel plants (even for just a few hours) is one of the points of the whole 'building renewable energy' thing. The problem is a bit more subtle; most gas plants are built in the expectation that they can operate for a certain number of hours per year and collect certain power prices for their output, every year for 25 years. When renewables are added to the mix through subsidies, these expectations are disappointed, and since gas plants incur startup and maintenance costs the owner may want to shut them down and certainly not build new ones. This may be fine, but may cause problems for the few hours per year when wind and solar is not available. It is therefore a reason for a regulator to offer the owners of gas and coal plants 'capacity payments' to keep the power plants online. Russia's power grid is almost entirely supported by capacity payments, with the result that power prices on the Russian spot markets are very low (around $20/MWh).

# Chapter 11

# Networking and Other Stuff
# Not Taught at State Schools

One of the things I find hardest about the world of work — and, specifically, business rather than academia — is knowing how to behave in certain situations. Some people find this easy, some feel really awkward at the intersection of professional and social behaviour. Maybe that's not you, in which case, lucky you. There is probably a class element to it, as well.

## 11.1. Networking Basics

Networking is an odd institution where you act as if you are meeting socially but it is actually about work. You exchange business cards, find out what other people do, show polite interest, use their name, and send a follow-up email. The email is not considered weird or binding, a simple 'nice to meet you' with some indication you remember what was discussed and would like to remain in touch. You don't have to go with a list of key aims and make a beeline for the right people — you might be better off simply having a mental list of questions and a curious mind.

Usually a networking event is sponsored by a company which provides alcoholic beverages and, if you are lucky, canapes. It is considered bad form to scoff all the canapes and mainline the beverages.

Wear a jacket with two pockets, or have a handbag with two sections. This is for business cards. One pocket is for your cards, the other for those of other people. Exchanging business cards in the West is awkward enough already, since there is no protocol and sometimes you find yourself clutching your card nervously while the other person shows no sign of going for theirs (or that may just be me). In most of Asia, there is protocol — you hold your business card carefully in both hands and extend it to them, and then take theirs and study it for a few moments, ideally saying something about it, like repeating their title in a thoughtful voice. This is a really easy habit to get into, so you can basically use it anywhere, and if you do this in the West people will say "oh, you must have spent time in Asia" and you can smile and look cosmopolitan even if you haven't. In Japan it is quite hard not to mirror the small head-dip bow people do (we are a species with a strong drive to imitate one another's behaviour), but I am told by my Japanese colleagues that bowing looks stupid on Westerners, or specifically on me, and is not expected.

There are three difficult parts of networking. The first is remembering people's names and faces, which I am terrible at (and it is really obvious if you only use their name after reading their badge). The second is making good conversation, of which we discuss more later. The third is escaping a conversation which has run its course with grace and elegance, ideally without then wandering the room looking desperately for someone else to talk to (this is a good time to visit the bathroom so it doesn't look like you were desperate to ditch them with no replacement conversationalist lined up. Unfortunately, there are only so many times you can reasonably visit the bathroom in a given timeframe).

Sometimes you do end up talking with someone you have nothing in common with, and awkwardly discussing the weather/cities/favourite restaurants/things to do locally. This can be OK too, it is a normal part of networking (my husband reads about football and cricket partly to have something to say). My colleague and super-networker Benjamin Kafri reads the Economist partly to have a short list of relevant topics to touch on, where he is not completely ignorant but would not claim native knowledge, although his true skill is remembering everything about everyone he meets. He can ask a person how the restaurant he recommended to them a year ago at a similar event was. He remembers if they like skiing or snowboarding. (A lot of people like one or the other. It is the sort of thing people in finance do. I just point out that in my opinion it is an expensive way to break one's legs and therefore better avoided, thus inviting the group to exchange their extensive repertoire of snowsport injury stories and think me a fantastic conversationalist for nodding along).

Ideally though, you talk work, because that is what you are both there for. It's always safe to ask people what they do at their company, and if you don't know the company, about what the company does. Often this is boring, long and hard to follow. I find it helps, particularly with people keen to tell you about their business model at length, to adopt an innocent expression and ask "so how does that make money?" This often gets to the heart of what they do. "So who pays you for that?" is another good one in the same vein. If you don't ask these questions, you can spend half an hour listening to someone talk proudly about their business, and not have the foggiest idea of who their customers are and what they sell. People are generally happy to answer questions that are a genuine attempt to reduce ignorance.

Also, high heels. Don't wear them unless you can stand around in them for hours, because sitting down is not an option unless you find someone absolutely fascinating.

## 11.2.  Being Female — Pros and Cons

As far as I can tell, as a female professional I am supposed to act like a role model for more junior women. I find this obligation awkward and uncomfortable, mainly because I have never experienced direct or definite negative discrimination for not having a Y-chromosome, and have almost certainly benefitted from positive discrimination when conference organisers are putting together a programme of speakers.

I recognise that this is a litany of privilege, but my point is that if you are a young woman starting out, it's not necessarily going to be awful for you — and good people exist. Both Michael Liebreich and Bloomberg the company make considerable efforts to ensure that women in their businesses succeed on their merits. Whatever the toxic culture of parts of the world, parts of business are well ahead and it's now embarrassing to have a boardroom, office or panel debate composed entirely of men.

Nonetheless… it's noticeable how many fewer women there are, the higher you go in most organisations. When one tries to put together a panel discussion and get some kind of gender mix, it is normally necessary to invite many more women than men to get the same number of acceptances (and senior women are rarer, hence harder to find to invite). My colleague William Young says that when inviting speakers to a major conference, about two out of three male speakers accept the invitation, compared with one in two invited women. My theory is that women are more likely than men to consider the merits of giving a conference presentation versus a day in the office getting some work done, and decide in favour of the work.

The reasons why an individual woman doesn't end up in a senior role are different but often very rational. Anecdotally, it seems as if women are more likely to move country and take a career hit when following a male partner's job. It also appears to me that female professionals respond to feeling underpaid, underappreciated, or not making progress in their current job by seeking a new job — while their male counterparts more often express their dissatisfaction to their manager first, which makes the manager more alert for opportunities to move or promote them. Complaining doesn't always get what you want and can be overused, but it's more likely to change things positively than saying nothing until the day you announce your resignation and move to another company, where you'll need to prove yourself over again. Maybe I've just had great managers, but I would recommend people of all genders be honest with their manager if they're not happy with something at work.

There is always the odd awkward moment — a man three times my age hitting on me when I thought I was interviewing him — and I admit that aged 24 I cut my hair very short in the hopes of being taken more seriously, and am generally quite dowdy. It may have helped (but other young women should wear whatever they feel comfortable with and cut their hair however they like). I have only three pieces of sartorial advice. Firstly, if you wear dresses, there are some very nice ones available that are machine washable, and those will save you a small fortune in dry cleaning bills and are also better for the environment. Secondly, buy suit jackets with two pockets, one for your business cards and one for other people's, because it is embarrassing to fumble around through a stack to give someone your card. Thirdly, new suit jackets always have the pockets sewn up and you are meant to unpick them after purchase, apparently this is one of those things that people go to private school to learn.

I think I get asked to chair or to moderate panel discussions much more often than an equivalently talented man would, because I am a woman. This is probably due to the laudable desire of conference organisers to avoid all-male lineups. Unfortunately, while moderating panels is a good gig for an analyst — we get to ask the smart questions — chairing an event is deadly dull; one has to try to memorise the biographies of a bunch of mostly-male speakers, explain where the toilets are, and stand there looking attentive a lot. This is a lot of work and fails to demonstrate to the audience that one has anything to say, so these days I politely decline such invitations. It's not much of a step forward for the representation of women in business if we are standing there introducing the content speakers, and also, I am really bad at it.

I don't have a solution to the visible gender gap at the higher levels of organisations. Women should look out for one another, but not to the extent of taking on an extra burden in comparison to men. But we have at least come a long way. Read Sheryl Sandberg's *Lean In* for better advice — or at least follow her suggestions that you should choose a partner (if you want a partner) who will support your career as much as they expect you to support theirs, that you shouldn't dial back on your professional ambitions now because in the next 5 years you may have a baby ('don't leave before you leave'), and be part of an important meeting, conference or conversation whenever you have a chance, while ducking out of unimportant ones — it's OK to have better things to do.

## 11.3. Job Interviews

I have been the interviewer many more times than I have been interviewed, and so there are much better sources for general tips on how to get a job. Get someone to proofread your CV before you send it, wear clean clothes, be on time, and don't start your cover letter to, say, Bloomberg with reasons why you want to work for McKinsey (this happens). We know you're not writing your best enthusiastic prose solely for our benefit, but a lack of attention to detail is not a good sign.

The people screening CVs and conducting interviews are human too. In general, one cannot interview all applicants — that would be a waste of everyone's time — and one wants to interview a diverse sample of the best. So one sighs with relief when an otherwise quite decent CV has a typo, or the cover letter starts Dear Sirs — it means one fewer thing to read carefully before making the difficult decision about whether it is worth one's own and the candidate's time to conduct an interview. Incidentally, don't misgender people, they hate it (it's hilarious to respond to a man who starts a general email Dear Sirs with 'Dear Madam', though. I really recommend it as proportionate retribution). There are perfectly good non-gendered forms of address — 'To whom it may concern', 'Dear hiring team', or 'Dear [full name]' if you know the name but are not sure of their pronoun.

Once in interview, good candidates make several bad and completely avoidable mistakes.

The first mistake is thinking that interviewers care about the answer to the warm-up question — a starting question about something the candidate really should know about, like why they are applying for the job or why they studied a particular course. This question is supposed to put the candidate at their ease. The answer should be appropriate, but brief. The candidate will get no marks by talking about their passion for environmental sciences for 15 min and leaving no time for difficult questions. Candidates basically start with zero marks and score for insightful answers, so blathering about your passion just wastes your time to impress. We have dozens of passionate and pleasant applicants and we couldn't hire them all if we wanted to, so we really do need to get to the point — which is whether an applicant would be good at the job.

Another common mistake is panicking when applicants do not know the answer to a numerical or analytical question immediately. Generally speaking, the interviewer does not expect anyone to. The idea is to see that the candidate does not panic, and is able to think and approach the question logically, asking for clarification. This makes sense — in the workplace you generally will not know how to do everything, it is far more important that you apply good reasoning skills to a problem when it arises.

Listen to the questions, and do not be afraid to pause for breath. The interviewer will probably have a list of questions for all candidates, to compare answers as fairly as possible. If the interviewer is trying to interrupt with questions, they are probably trying to steer the candidate back towards something that would actually credit them. It is wise to ask an interviewer 'is this what you are looking for?' or 'should I go on?' rather than making them cut you off; nobody wants to work with someone who will not listen.

Things that are worth doing if applying for a job: have a two-line version of any relevant thesis or publication mentally prepared, and any surprising findings. Know what the company you are applying for does, and have a quick google of the interviewers, if you know their names. Get any interview practice you can, to be focused but relaxed on the day. Send one or two emails asking what has happened to your application if you do not hear back for months, but do not cold email an entire company.

Good luck. From an interviewer's standpoint, the decision is always very difficult and we often want to hire everyone we meet, while also needing to interview everyone we have chosen to interview before making an offer. This is often why communication takes time. Sorry.

## 11.4. Advice from Other People to Those Wanting a Job in Clean Energy

I asked the various clean energy finance professionals that I spoke to for this book (in 2018) what advice they would give anyone looking to work in the sector. Here is a selection of what they said.

Charles Yonts, an equity analyst — someone who tracks the rise and fall of stock market-quoted companies and issues buy and sell recommendations: "Remember that solar panels are a commodity, so equities will trade and valuations fluctuate with demand and supply, moving in cycles just like they do in cement, steel and property. What is astounding is that even quite experienced investors fall into the trap of thinking that given the phenomenal secular growth in solar, it will somehow be immune from these cyclical patterns, and then they get destroyed. The flip side of this is that when we enter the down phase of the cycle, there is an up on the other side."

Belén Gallego, an entrepreneur and co-founder and CEO of consulting firm ATA Insights, said "We [the clean energy industry] need all the help we can get! There is not always much money in renewables, but you can still forge your own path."

Dr Zhengrong Shi, who built a company from nothing and was at one point one of the richest people in China (more details on Suntech in Chapter 13), says that early stage companies should not try to do everything and should be happy to take on small chunks of business. "I see startups that I work with get overexcited about 1–2 million dollar contracts" he says. "But it's good to get small orders that are not so high risk. Also, don't try to sell a product before it is good".

# Chapter 12

# Solar After the 2008 Crash: Finding a New Normal

When the Spanish solar market hit its deadline in 2008, a global financial crisis was in full swing. The US subprime mortgage market collapsed in 2007, and the investment bank Lehman Brothers filed for bankruptcy on September 15, 2008. The financial crisis was widely blamed for the crash in solar module prices, but as far as I can tell had little to do with it — the prices of physical modules (as opposed to the stock prices of companies) fell simply because supply grew faster than demand, as new factories came online. Annual new build volumes continued to hit a new record every year, and annual investment figures hardly saw a dent; the problem was a fundamental oversupply of every part of the solar value chain. The financial crisis almost certainly had a role in the fall in solar stock prices which made it more difficult for solar manufacturing companies to sell more shares and raise more money, but that was a secondary effect as most were not in an expansion phase anyway.

## 12.1. Manufacturers

After 2008, solar manufacturers went through a 5-year period of losing money, and a great many went bankrupt. New polysilicon factories came online, and the price of polysilicon dropped steadily, from over $400/kg in 2008 to under $20/kg in 2013 — barely the marginal cost of making polysilicon, never mind paying polysilicon companies back for the capital they invested in factories (as of early 2019, it's around $10/kg as most manufacturers have reduced their costs even further). The price under long-term contracts was still around $60/kg, and so the lawyers for the companies buying polysilicon scanned the contracts desperately looking for loopholes. In some cases they found them; in many, the buyers got out of the long-term contracts by the time-honoured method of going bankrupt; in some cases the two companies negotiated a deal where the seller accepted lower prices than originally agreed, in exchange for the customer continuing to exist.

Firms competed with each other fiercely to sell solar modules. Manufacturers which had made improvements in technology and cost reduced prices and stayed afloat, while those which had coasted on long-term polysilicon contracts and high module prices went bust. "When the tide goes out, you see who is swimming naked", as investor Warren Buffett famously described this situation.

One example was BP Solar. Several oil companies have attempted solar manufacturing in the past, and given up after a few years; for example, Shell sold its solar division to German solar manufacturer SolarWorld in 2006. Oil companies come in for a lot of criticism from activist shareholders and environmental lobbyists for quitting solar manufacturing. In my view, this is not wholly rational, as there are no synergies between the two businesses.

Since synergies is an overrated word, it may be worth using an analogy: take a busy blacksmith in a medieval village where the children go without shoes. Should she go into the shoemaking business? It depends. If shoemaking requires much the same tools and skills as blacksmithing, there are synergies and perhaps she should take an apprentice and expand her forge. On the other hand, if it would require her to retrain and crowd her forge with new equipment, she might find that her new business venture left the village's tools unmade, horses unshod, and her purse empty. In this case, perhaps someone else in the village should go and apprentice with a shoemaker elsewhere, and come back to set up a shop. If there are no synergies, the blacksmith and shoemaker will most likely serve the village better and at a lower cost if they stay independent. (The shoemaker could always ask nicely to borrow the blacksmith's forge if he needs a hot awl occasionally.)

Oil companies are good at finding oil, negotiating agreements with governments to get it out of the ground, and then getting it out and transporting it around. Solar manufacturers need to be good at continuously improving production processes, managing supply chains and inventory, and marketing. There are no major synergies, which is why no oil company has become a leading solar manufacturer since the industry reached a significant scale. (Outside manufacturing, oil companies do have some advantages. Some have made investments in solar and wind projects, and many have biofuel interests for obvious reasons. There are some synergies in relationships with governments in emerging markets, helping first-of-their-kind projects secure a promise to pay for the power. Oil companies may also have some relevant expertise in building and maintaining offshore infrastructure like offshore wind projects.)

There is occasionally an attempt to make oil companies invest in renewables as a moral imperative. However, when we buy oil, we are treating it as a necessary evil; we shouldn't expect oil companies to operate in a business they are bad at as well, using oil wealth to compete with companies which are actually good at solar. The problem for solar manufacturers is that there are always new entrants trying to be the next big player, causing near-continuous oversupply and vicious competition. Pumping oil is much easier than staying a fraction ahead on manufacturing costs, but it doesn't really make much sense to cross-subsidise one activity with the other — and in one logical extreme would result in an oil company's solar division which literally could not fail, pushing out more innovative pure solar companies.

One casualty after 2008 was Massachusetts-based Evergreen Solar, which had a 'string ribbon' solar wafer making technology that in theory could cut costs, by drawing wafers directly from molten silicon rather than slicing. Unfortunately, it had long-term contracts to buy silicon at prices that had looked good in 2007–2008, but were ruinously expensive in 2010. Evergreen Solar went bankrupt in 2011.

A lot of the blame for the module price crash was directed at the Chinese companies, which had built the largest factories in the world, often buying European or US-designed manufacturing equipment. Firms like Suntech, Yingli Solar, Trina Solar, JA Solar, Jinko, China Sunergy, LDK, Renesola and GCL were some of the largest manufacturers, and were able to offer some of the lowest prices on the market (although higher than the prices some of their less well-known competitors offered out of desperation). Initially, their European and US competitors tried claiming that Chinese modules were all poor quality, but this was not supported by laboratory or field tests. It is true that the pricing pressure led to some firms cutting corners — using substandard encapsulant and back-sheet materials, for example, which degrade more quickly than the rest of the module and ruin either the transparent front or the waterproof back. There were almost too many small Chinese module manufacturers to name — at the annual Shanghai New Energy Conference in 2008, there were hundreds of stands representing companies with names like Zhejiang Sunlight Systems or Jiangsu Apollo. Of 568 exhibitors (according to the online catalogue), most were small module makers. Of course not all of them were meeting the highest standards of material sourcing and fabrication — they were teetering on the edge of bankruptcy too. How was a module buyer to know which products were well made?

It's difficult to argue the value of advertising from a perspective of social good, but there is one way in which it can be done. Generally, if a company spends significant amounts of money promoting a branded product, it's likely to pay at least some attention to the consistency of the product — probably more than a firm which has no reputation to protect. If you bought a bad can of Coca Cola, you'd be far more disappointed and remember the experience better than if you bought an unbranded cola-flavoured drink that turned out to be bad. For this reason, it can be logical to buy from a company which spends money promoting its products, even if smaller companies offer what appears to be the same quality product at a lower price. This can be done by having an eye-catching booth at a trade show, by sponsoring conferences and buying advertisements in trade magazines, and even by advertising in mainstream media or sports. For example, Trina Solar sponsored the Renault car team for the Formula One racing event in 2010, while Yingli sponsored the football World Cup in 2010, spending an estimated $30–40 million. It is not clear if any customer specifically requested Trina or Yingli modules as a result of this promotion; one suspects that this sort of advertising is good for the ego of the upper management, independent of its effect on the bottom line.

The first major consolidation phase of solar module manufacturing ran from 2008 to about 2012, and bankruptcy claimed large companies as well as many with names that are variants on Solar Power Systems (originality in naming has not been a notable feature of the solar industry to date).

## 12.2.  Developers — Making Hay While the Sun Shone

The module price crash created huge opportunity for the companies which financed, developed and built solar power plants. If they were lucky with the timing, they signed power price contracts or got feed-in tariffs locked in before the module price crash, and got to keep the price difference as profit margin. In places where solar power plants were built under contract with customers, like the US, developers could start to offer much lower power prices which appealed to more customers, and begin to scale up their ambitions from a relatively small base. This was a payoff for years of work for some firms, like Jigar Shah's SunEdison. This company pioneered a business model of offering 25-year power purchase agreements to owners of large roofs, at prices which made immediate financial sense, with the payments going to external investors who had paid for the project.

Jigar Shah, founder of SunEdison, remembers, "In 2003, our model was an immediate hit with customers, and we signed up [high-end US supermarket chain] Whole Foods, [office supplies chain] Staples and [furniture store] IKEA within six months. The customers said, the cost of one of these solar projects is the same as a brand new store. We're building two stores every month right now, why would I divert this money to solar systems instead? And they signed power purchase agreements."

The challenge was initially finding investors willing to take the bet on solar tech working, and some of SunEdison's first customers had to wait 2 years after signing up until the company found investors. Jigar Shah funded the first project on his credit card, and other early projects used capital from wealthy individuals.

Investors naturally had many questions about this new asset class, and not all of them could be answered based on past experience. Shah remembers, "Goldman Sachs asked, 'what is the residual value of these panels?

What can you resell them for after the 25 years?' And I scoured the internet and found only about 12 transactions."

In June 2005, Goldman Sachs agreed to fund the first solar project with SunEdison. "People were more interested when Goldman came in, but we still needed to pay 'trust brokers' – individuals who vouched for us and had a knack for exclusive transactions. We paid syndication fees to one particular broker, who specialised in rolling stock – trucks, trains, etc. — for municipal and state governments, and had a record of bringing banks transactions that they liked. He helped us get one deal done with a low-level agent for Wells Fargo out of Minneapolis, who ran the division leasing diesel generators and other equipment. This avoided the top guy at Wells Fargo, who believed solar was too risky for leasing finance (and did not know they had done a solar transaction until 8 months later). Wells Fargo's holding company was making 11–12% return from solar and wind investments, but we got financing at 4.6% interest from the same company's leasing division. We never disappointed them though. We made all the payments on time".

By 2008, SunEdison was one of the largest solar companies in the US and had bought six smaller engineering contractors, and banks were becoming comfortable with lending to projects using experienced contractors (like SunEdison). It was able to scale up rapidly in 2009, moving into markets like Italy and Canada. It claimed a then-ambitious pipeline of 1.5 GW of projects in plan, when in November 2009 it was bought by polysilicon maker MEMC for $200 million. MEMC made SunEdison the main growth driver of the company, even changing its name to SunEdison (more about further developments, including bankruptcy, in the following chapter). Jigar Shah, the founder, left to pursue other opportunities and now runs an investment firm called Generate Capital.

# Chapter 13

# Solar Failures 2009–2013: Case Studies

It's always easy to point at mistakes made by executives and companies with the benefit of hindsight, but the people managing solar manufacturers after the 2008 crash in global prices were in a very difficult situation. The selling price of modules was often below the cost of production, and the main way to improve cost of production is by expanding production volume and setting up new, technologically advanced factories. The economically logical alternative, simply to shut down until the module price went up, would probably be the end of the company as competitors would continue to expand and bring their costs down. Large firms which had invested in their brand were unwilling to do this. About the only good way forward for manufacturers was to start developing and building their own solar power plants, to capture some of the margin they were losing to competition on module sales.

It is a dangerous fallacy that simply expanding into a new part of the value chain will always add value to a company. A company's value is based on its return on capital employed, as well as its growth, and going into a new sector only makes sense if the return on capital employed in the new sector is at least as high as the return on its existing businesses. A company's return on capital employed depends on the profit, divided by the amount of money it has invested in its operations. When your existing business of solar module making is generating horribly negative returns, it can't really hurt to go into a part of the value chain where returns are positive — unless you do it very badly.

## 13.1. Suntech

Suntech Power Holdings was the first Chinese solar company to file for a US Initial Public Offering, on the New York stock exchange, in 2005. It grew to become the world's largest solar module manufacturer in 2010 and 2011, and was one of the best known and respected of the Chinese brands. Its charismatic and affable founder and CEO, Dr Zhengrong Shi (Shi is his family name, and under Chinese convention would appear first), studied at the University of New South Wales, Australia, under Professor Martin Green, still a world-leading academic researcher on solar technology. In 2001, Dr Shi returned to China to found Suntech, and by 2005 was one of China's richest men, with glowing newspaper articles about the 'Sun King'.

To many at the time, Suntech symbolised the best of Western technology in partnership with Chinese industrial efficiency. Professor Green, speaking in July 2018, credits the firm with bringing real expertise in cell technology (not just module assembly) to China for the first time, and accelerating cost reductions for the whole industry.

Like most solar manufacturers, Suntech made losses between 2008 and 2012 due to the oversupply of modules. Dr Shi himself went on a roadshow for investors and banks, explaining the technical edge Suntech had with the aim of differentiating Suntech's product and asking a higher price. (I attended one of these roadshows, and learned a lot about solar manufacturing technology — Dr Shi was generous with his time on follow-up questions, quite beyond a sales pitch. It was obvious even then that he was more interested in the technology than in the money.) Suntech had raised a $541 million convertible bond (i.e. it borrowed money which could be repaid in cash or converted into stock) in 2007, due on March 15, 2013.

Suntech was ahead of many of its competitors in realising that the market for modules would crash and that it should diversify. In June 2008, it took control of Global Solar Fund (GSF), which invested in PV projects in Spain and Italy. In May 2010, Suntech guaranteed a financing arrangement of 554 million euros by China Commercial Bank to GSF and related companies, using 560 million euros of German government bonds held by GSF Capital as collateral.

As the market got worse in early 2012, Suntech tried to sell GSF to raise cash, but 'uncovered irregularities' during its internal due diligence.

On July 30, 2012, Suntech admitted that it had investigated and found out that the German bonds used as collateral did not exist. This was embarrassing, and Suntech's stock price fell 41%. Dr Shi was removed as CEO in August 2012, although remained in the non-executive role of Chairman, and was still a majority owner of the company. The bizarre case of the non-existent bonds was settled in March 2013 without GSF directors admitting liability. Dr Shi was still listed on the entrepreneur magazine Hurun Report's China Rich List for 2013, with wealth of $300 million — albeit mostly tied up in Suntech stock.

Later in March 2013, Suntech's convertible loan came due, and the company did not have the cash to pay it. Although it attempted to negotiate a delayed settlement, it was forced to file for bankruptcy on March 20, 2013.

In September and October 2013, Italian courts ordered the seizure of 47 solar plants, totalling 37.8 MW, owned by GSF (i.e. Suntech), due to what it described as potentially fraudulent permitting and planning. This did not increase the chances of Suntech finding a way to negotiate bankruptcy as an independent company.

In November 2013, the local government in Suntech's home province of Wuxi found an acceptable way to keep the factories running and not lose the local jobs: Hong Kong-listed manufacturer Shunfeng Photovoltaic — formerly a very minor player compared with Suntech — took it over. Most of Suntech's many creditors were forced to accept just under a third of the money they were owed, since no better options were available.

Suntech's fall shows that diversifying downstream in the value chain is not always a safe bet, especially when a firm with manufacturing expertise plays in the tricky world of Italian paperwork. Dr Shi, speaking with hindsight in July 2018, says of the company's fall that "We were cheated by a bad person [at GSF]. We knew this guy for 3 years, but sometimes people can change. However, there should have been no risk to the financing — for all the assets guaranteed, we had the project itself as collateral, there were three layers of security." The German bonds were never called upon. "Once we discovered that we were cheated, we willingly disclosed this to Wall Street. That triggered panic selling and the stock price fell, and the Board of Directors said someone had to be sacrificed for the board to save face." That someone was Dr Shi.

This move to save face was counterproductive, he says. To build the company, Dr Shi had forged strong ties of trust with Chinese banks and local governments, and the Board — including David King, former Chief Finance Officer, who became CEO — had not. "Once I was removed, they hired a basic team to run the firm" he says. "David King had never lived in China, did not speak Mandarin, did not understand the way of doing things in China. The only thing the board could do was threaten and blackmail the government and banks that if they did not do such-and-such the company would go bankrupt." The Chinese authorities did not act to rescue the company under its American-style new management, and instead it was sold at a knockdown price to new management under Shunfeng.

After Suntech went bankrupt, Dr Shi was free, though times were tough as media reported that he was under investigation by the Chinese financial service authorities. He was still the largest shareholder, and in China it is often assumed that the largest shareholder has operational responsibility — but he had no authority over the company's decisions after being removed as Chairman in April 2013. "I would have been put in jail many times if I had done all the things that media said I did! But I had just trusted the wrong people" he says.

He was cleared of deliberate wrongdoing, and was free to move to Sydney. After 10 years of living the CEO lifestyle of constant travel, chauffeuring and everything being arranged for him, he spent four months learning to drive, to shop and to cook. "I could have eaten out every evening with friends, but I cooked alone, and after a few weeks I was so happy and confident. I lost 10 kg and finally had my body back!"

Dr Shi is now an adjunct professor at the University of New South Wales, and has a number of investments in solar companies. He is particularly involved on the technical side of a new company, SunMan, making semi-flexible crystalline silicon PV panels under the brand name eArche.

Suntech is back in operation as part of Shunfeng. It no longer has an outstanding reputation for technological leadership among solar cell makers, but is still a major cell and module manufacturer with a brand respected for quality.

## 13.2. Solyndra

Solyndra was a Silicon Valley-based company making solar panels comprised of racks of tubes with copper indium gallium selenide thin-film photovoltaic coating. The idea was that they were lightweight and had low wind resistance relative to normal solid modules, so could be installed on commercial roofs too weak for conventional solar. Best of all, they didn't use silicon, which at the time the company was seeking to scale up, was spiking in price to over \$400/kg. In 2009, Solyndra reported a module selling price of \$3.29/W, about 80 cents/W more expensive than crystalline silicon but potentially easier to install — not too unsound an economic proposition. Several German firms were major customers, as the German feed-in tariffs were good and some German roofs are not suitable for normal modules. The argument Solyndra made was that these roofs would never be suitable for normal modules and therefore there would always be a market for an alternative product (this argument is still made today by makers of niche products).

In March 2009, Solyndra was awarded a \$535 million loan guarantee from the US Department of Energy, as part of the '1705' economic stimulus programme intended to restart growth after the 2008 financial crash. The Federal Financing Bank provided the money, to be used to construct a second factory making 250 MW of modules per year. In addition, Solyndra raised nearly \$1.2 billion from venture capital investors including Argonaut Private Equity, Rockport Capital, Redpoint Ventures and Abu Dhabi state venture Masdar.

In August 2011, Solyndra ceased operations and shortly afterwards filed for bankruptcy. Many of its manufacturing assets were sold at auction, but little of the investors or government money was recovered. The firm had simply been unable to sell as the crystalline silicon module price dropped; in 2009 it had been competing with crystalline silicon modules at around \$2.00/W, but by late 2011 the crystalline silicon module price was around \$1.40/W. German tariffs had been reduced in line with the reduction in photovoltaic costs, exposing the fallacy of the 'niche market' argument; it was not economically viable to install Solyndra modules under the new, lower tariffs and increasing the tariffs again would have over-rewarded normal solar, even if the government had wanted to do it. Solyndra had no workable pathway to bringing cost down to a competitive level and swiftly ran out of cash.

The Solyndra debacle was the trigger for many recriminations, particularly towards the US Department of Energy for using federal money to back a loser. The process of awarding the loan guarantee was examined and concerns expressed about transparency and corruption, but ultimately nothing too scandalous was uncovered. The US government had simply decided to take a risk it expected to have a strategic payout, and along with the private investors, lost.

The firm was not the first or last expensive thin-film failure; for a while, Silicon Valley venture capital investors seemed to feel that they all needed a thin-film company in their portfolio in case thin-film was The Next Big Thing (more in Chapter 18). This kind of group think is not unusual among humans.

Some companies were worse than legitimate businesses which made bad decisions.

## 13.3. Hanergy

Hanergy is a case study of a solar company playing in the murkier areas of stock market fundraising and local development finance. Whenever there is enormous enthusiasm for a particular product or technology, there can be firms taking advantage to raise money beyond their ability to deliver on promises.

To begin near the end of the story, the market capitalisation of Hanergy Thin Film Power Group (ticker: 566) started rising for no obvious reason from \$4.4 billion in July 2014, and hit \$34 billion on the Hong Kong stock exchange in March 2015 (see Figure 13.1). The market capitalisation stayed around this level until May 20, 2015, when the company's valuation plunged \$19 billion in 30 minutes and it requested that

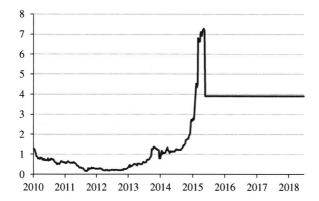

Figure 13.1.   Stock price of Hanergy Thin Film, January 1, 2010 to June 29, 2018.

trading be suspended. The Hong Kong Securities and Futures Commission ruled that trading would remain suspended while it investigated the company. As of late 2018, trading is still suspended.

Hanergy Holdings was founded in 1994, and developed a number of hydroelectric dams in rural China, in partnership with local government. In July 2009, the company entered solar with a reportedly $4 billion research and development centre for thin-film silicon solar technology in Heyuan, Guangdong, China. The founder, Li Hejun, had a history of entering industries where government funding was available for local projects, of which the hydro projects were the only notable success. He had very ostentatious offices at a former nightclub on the Beijing Olympic Park, designed to impress government officials and other visitors and encourage them to commit capital to his ventures.

In May 2010, Hanergy Holdings went through a complex transaction by which it became both investor and customer to Hong Kong-listed thin film silicon solar tech company Apollo Solar. Apollo was renamed Hanergy Thin Film (HTF), because it really helps with clear reporting when both sides of a contract have the same name. Hanergy Holdings agreed to buy $2.6 billion of manufacturing equipment from HTF.

An article titled *Blinded by Hanergy's Light*, by media group Caixin in December 2012, detailed substantial local government loans and financing that Hanergy took, in exchange for promising investments in factories and projects that would create local jobs. These investments either did not materialize or were downsized, and since all factories were supposedly using HTF equipment, much of the investment was booked as revenue by HTF. There was also a 30 billion yuan ($4.5 billion) credit line extended by China Development Bank for projects, although this was probably not fully used (similar credit lines to other solar companies with the China Development Bank were quietly cut off when the market deteriorated).

Lucy Hornby of the Financial Times in Beijing points out that, "this intersects on a much bigger issue outside solar power finance, the relationship between Chinese companies and their Hong Kong-listed subsidiaries. Sometimes mainland Chinese window-dress the results of the Hong Kong-listed subsidiary by stuffing any bad news into the unlisted operating companies." She explains that this boosts the Hong Kong company's stock price and may enable it to raise further financing more easily, by making the listed company appear more attractive than the corporation viewed as a whole. By any standards, however, HTF was unusually reliant on reporting revenue from Hanergy Holdings and appeared to have no sales to unrelated companies.

Hanergy Holdings then issued regular updates on the construction of factories in China's Haikou, Shuangli, Wujin, Changxing, Yucheng and Heyuan districts or cities, using the equipment. These updates did not include claims of actual production. In November 2012, Hanergy Holdings said that it had 3 GW of annual thin-film silicon solar module manufacturing technology, which would have been very impressive if it really existed and functioned. There were few reports of Hanergy modules being seen in the field, although we saw a few samples at trade shows. Nowhere near 3 GW/year could have been produced, because that volume would have shown up in the market somewhere. It is very common for manufacturing companies to report greater factory capacity than is actually in production at the time, but in Hanergy's case the discrepancy was very large indeed.

In 2013, the firm went on a technology buying spree, acquiring thin-film companies in Europe and the US that had been developed using large amounts of venture capital (Miasole had raised $495 million). The entire portfolio — Solibro, Miasole, Global Solar Energy and Alta Devices — cost about $200 million and definitely existed. Hanergy also bought UK solar installer Engensa, which definitely existed and sold products through the Swedish home shop IKEA. In 2013, I visited Hanergy Solar's stall in IKEA in Zurich and got a quote for getting my house fitted with solar (it seemed a little expensive and the subsidy regime at the time did not justify solar, but it was legitimate enough).

In 2014, Hanergy's stock price climbed steadily for no obvious reason. From July 2014 to March 2015, its market capitalisation rose from $4.4 billion to $34 billion. CEO Li Hejun was listed by Forbes in October 2014 as China's richest man, due to the value of HTF stock he held. The company's reported revenues and profits still seemed to be entirely due to HTF selling manufacturing equipment to Hanergy Holdings, however, and there was still no evidence that Hanergy Holdings was using the manufacturing equipment to make modules. A few journalists including Lucy Hornby at the Financial Times and a team at Caixin Global, me and an equity analyst called Charles Yonts seemed to be the main people publishing output sceptical about the stock price rise.

Although few equity analysts covered the stock, it was included in several indices tracking the general clean energy market (including some selected by BloombergNEF. When you are constructing an index of quoted companies to track a sector, you are trying to choose a diverse and representative range of companies in the sector, not pick winners). It was very thinly traded on the Hong Kong exchange and so very hard to short sell (short selling is an investment strategy used when you believe a stock price will fall. You borrow the stock from someone who owns it, for a small fee, and sell it, planning to buy it back at a lower price to return to the owners. You make money if you buy the stock back for less than you sold it for, minus the borrowing fees).

Financial Times analysis in March 2015 showed that HTF share prices "consistently surged late in the day, about 10 minutes before the exchange's close, from the start of 2013 to February [2015]… This means that an investor who held HTF shares from the start of trading at 9 am to 3:30 pm would have lost money – despite the company's share price rising by 1,168 percent between January 2013 and February 9, 2015." This does not conclusively prove that the share price was manipulated, but is unlikely to have occurred by chance.

In early 2015, I wrote a short note on the discrepancy between Hanergy's $34 billion valuation and that of its theoretical peers, First

Solar at $6.1 billion or Trina Solar at $1.1 billion (both companies which were definitely making and selling large volumes of solar panels).

Charles Yonts, looking back in June 2018 on sentiment from Hong Kong stock market investors during the rise, said "They were bemused. The reason that institutional fund managers were concerned was not that they wanted to hold the stock — anyone who looked at it even briefly felt assured that it wasn't something that they needed to own — but the problem was that Hanergy was in the indices which track the overall Hong Kong stock market [which rose due to Hanergy's presence]. How they are performing relative to the market is everything to a fund manager, and whatever they were doing, they were underperforming Hanergy, and getting questions from their bosses about that."

In May 2015, the HTF stock price crashed, and the Hong Kong stock exchange suspended trading while investigating the connected transactions between the legal entity Hanergy Holding, and HTF. This was complicated because, according to the Hong Kong Securities and Futures Commission, Hanergy Holding refused to supply documents. In September 2017 Li Hejun was barred from "serving as a director on the board of any company in Hong Kong for 8 years, after a court ruled that he was involved in misconduct related to the running of the former solar giant" (Bloomberg News, September 4, 2017). IKEA quietly switched to a different technology supplier.

As of July 2018, the Hong Kong stock exchange still lists Hanergy Thin Film as suspended, pending it meeting certain conditions including that it "disclose detailed information on the company, its activities, business, assets, liabilities, financial performance and prospects". The firm still sometimes issues press releases claiming technology breakthroughs, calling itself "the world's largest clean energy company" and occasionally describing Li Hejun — still barred from serving as a director for any company in Hong Kong — as CEO of the theoretically separate Chinese parent, Hanergy Holdings.

Li Hejun may still have support from some officials, suggests Lucy Hornby. "He pitches Chinese indigenism, Chinese environmentalism and Chinese technology leadership" she said in July 2018. "He still appeals to national priorities. It's also possible that his debt is so enormous that someone cannot afford to let him fail."

Charles Yonts sees no sign of progress. "Hanergy has been forgotten like a bad dream by Hong Kong investors" he says. "I don't see any trigger for a resolution."

## 13.4. SunEdison

SunEdison had a confusing history as a polysilicon manufacturer called MEMC, which acquired a rooftop solar project developer called SunEdison from its investors and from founder Jigar Shah in 2009, and from 2013 onwards made solar project development the focus of its business. The firm, then with a market capitalisation of $1.9 billion, raised debt and equity to acquire or develop pipelines of solar and wind projects around the world. It was extraordinarily ambitious, sending teams into India, Latin America and the Middle East to scout out project opportunities and buy options on land, as well as buying some successful wind project developers with pipelines. It even hired away one of BloombergNEF's researchers in Japan to find its solar projects to build there.

A recurring danger of project development is that costs occur well before revenue, and project developers tend not to have a large pile of cash to fall back on. The idea of being a project developer is that a firm will sell projects once they have been built to long-term investors, realising cash to reinvest in further projects — but if something goes wrong with this process, the developer can find itself owning a large number of half-finished projects but unable to pay its bills. Consequently, the timing of project sales is very important to developers.

In May 2014, SunEdison launched a 'yieldco' called TerraForm Power. Yieldcos are worth devoting some time to a further explanation.

There are various risks in investing in a renewable energy project. Most of them are risks about whether you will get your money or not — performance risk, payment risk, curtailment risk (this last is when the grid does not have enough capacity to take the energy your project is generating, so you lose it). If the project pays in a currency other than your own, there is currency risk — the project may pay a constant and reliable stream of rupees, for example, but they may be worth less of the dollars and euros that you needed to buy the equipment in the first place, and that you need to pay your staff or pay dividends to your investors. However, another form of risk is liquidity risk: you may need to get your investment out in a hurry, for example if you are an insurance firm that needs to make a big payout. This is a big problem if you have invested your money in buying a solar or wind project, because to get a good price when you sell it will take time — a buyer will want to do due diligence on all aspects of the project. Hence, many funds have a restriction on how much of their money they can invest in such 'illiquid assets' which cannot quickly be sold for a fair price.

Yieldcos are, fundamentally, a way of reducing liquidity risk to attract a larger pool of investors with a low cost of capital. The idea is that a yieldco owns a portfolio of simple cash-generating assets — solar projects or wind farms, for example, or electricity transmission lines. The yieldco is then listed on a stock exchange, and the shares traded. It releases regular, transparent results about how its portfolio is performing, and about projects it plans to buy. Investors hold stock in the yieldco, they expect dividends, and they can sell stock on the stock market if they need the cash in a hurry.

This is the classic model, used by European solar yieldcos such as Foresight, Bluefield and NextEnergy: launching traded funds which hold a fixed portfolio of solar projects and gave regular dividends. Sometimes they raise more money from new investors, buying further projects and increasing the revenues to remunerate the new investors. Occasionally, they might get ambitious, for example by renegotiating an operation and maintenance agreement downwards to increase return for shareholders slightly, or securing a loan at a lower rate of interest. But they were not intended to be high return or exciting investments.

One problem with American yieldcos around 2014 and 2015 was that they were being marketed as stocks with a high growth potential. Jigar Shah, who sold SunEdison in 2009, explains that "at the time, comparable companies like Canadian income trusts told their investors that they would grow at 3–5%/year, while the US solar yieldcos offered, at the low end, 8%/year and SunEdison — the most egregious offender — offered 20% growth per year". One reason for this was that US renewable energy yieldcos could enjoy tax advantages if they kept adding more projects to their portfolios. However, outside the tax structure, it should have been clear to investors that growing a project portfolio without either further investment or taking risk was not possible. In any case, the promise of growth was alluring to investors, but created a constant need within the yieldcos for more projects.

SunEdison's new yieldco, TerraForm Power, also started out on the hunt for projects — but it had an additional problem. Six out of twelve of TerraForm's advisory board members were also on SunEdison's board, and the projects bought by TerraForm were being sold by SunEdison. The setup was not unusual at the time — Spanish construction and infrastructure firm Abengoa had a similar arrangement with its own yieldco, Abengoa Yield and US manufacturer — developers SunPower and First Solar worked together with a vehicle called 8point3energy (light takes 8.3 min to travel from the Sun to the Earth). A few investors pointed out the possible risks of a company transferring assets from itself, to a vehicle controlled by itself but owned by external investors. The obvious risk is that the price paid by the yieldco (and therefore ultimately by investors) might be more than the project is really worth.

For the first 2 years, there was little evidence of any problems with developers using the yieldcos they controlled. In July 2015, SunEdison launched a second yieldco, TerraForm Global; while TerraForm Power was only investing in North American projects, TerraForm Global had a wider remit to buy SunEdison projects in the developing world.

In 2015, however, SunEdison was under some financial pressure. It had a lot of projects under construction, with suppliers and contractors demanding to be paid. Activist shareholders alleged that it was taking early payments from the TerraForms to meet its urgent requirements, and perhaps being optimistic about the assumptions used for valuing the projects being transferred to the TerraForms.

Stock prices may also have played a role in the company's poor decision-making. Soaring stock prices depressing the 'yield' of the yieldco (the yield is the annual dividend per share — a regular payout from cash-flow — divided by the stock price). Jigar Shah says that, "the yieldco was paying a dividend from its operating solar projects, but the yieldco's stock price went up so the yield went down. SunEdison made the mistake of thinking that people loved solar so much that they were willing to own the stock at a price which only paid a 3% dividend yield. So they said, our cost of capital has suddenly gone from about 7% to about 4%. To get our growth done, we can buy all of these assets at 4% return — including

TerraForm Power paying two billion dollars in 2015 for a portfolio of wind projects from developer Invenergy. So SunEdison had lost discipline and was overpaying for assets because it thought investors were fine with paying for growth at any cost. This was not true, and as soon as the investors figured it out, they sold stock."

"The assets were good, but the company had paid too much for them [see Chapter 14 for how to calculate the value of cash generating assets]. The firm raised more debt, which was easy to do using the high stock price and consequent valuation of 30 billion dollars." SunEdison's stock price fell 93% from July 2015 to March 2016, not because of any obvious market developments but simply because investors had lost trust in its model. This made banks which had lent SunEdison money nervous about its ability to repay. Already its interest payments were substantial — in the third quarter of 2015, SunEdison paid interest of $214 million and selling, general and admin expenses of $296 million on revenue of $476 million.

SunEdison came up with a hare-brained scheme to buy US rooftop firm Vivint Solar for $2.2 billion, which caused further unhappiness among activist shareholders (notably billionaire David Tepper, who filed an action to block the sale in February 2016). Vivint pulled out of the deal in March 2016 and SunEdison filed for bankruptcy in April 2016. Over the next 2 years, all SunEdison's assets were sold off piecemeal to other developers. The TerraForm yieldcos were bought in late 2017 by Canadian private equity fund Brookfield.

## 13.5. Conclusions on Solar Bankruptcies

The module oversupply of 2010–2013 left even some of the survivors, such as Yingli, with depleted balance sheets and high levels of debt. The grim truth is that making solar modules is never likely to be a very profitable business, and building bigger and bigger factories to drive down costs is a technique that works, but keeps margins tight. In this respect, it is similar to semiconductor manufacturing, where customers rather than most of the companies capture most of the value generated [Heck *et al.*, 2011].

Developing solar projects can be a profitable business, but missteps and miscalculations here can be just as dangerous as in any other segment.

# Chapter 14

# Project Finance and Calculating the Cost of Energy

Solar panels are sold in Watts, while energy is sold in kWh or MWh. This chapter aims to lay down the foundations of how to translate from one to the other, and explains Levelised Cost of Energy (LCOE) and why it varies.

## 14.1. The Cost of Capacity and the Cost of Generation (Buying a Car Versus Total Cost of Driving)

So far, we have mostly discussed the cost of solar photovoltaics in terms of dollars per W. This is because the per-W cost is the main feature of solar that is dependent on technology and can be quoted without a long discussion of the assumptions made. A Watt is just the capacity to produce electricity under standard (nearly optimal) conditions; real solar projects will only produce this much for a few hours per day (at most). The capacity in watts tells you how large the solar plant is.

Electricity is bought and sold in Wh (or, usually, kWh or MWh). So a relevant question is, how much does electricity from a solar plant cost per MWh? Unfortunately, this is not a simple question. (It is also not the only relevant question, but that complication will have to wait.)

A good analogy is that the cost per W is like the price of a car, while the cost per MWh (Levelised Cost of Energy, LCOE) is the cost of driving a car per km — including the cost of buying the car, interest on the car loan, fuel cost, insurance and maintenance. In the car analogy you may want to calculate this to decide whether you should buy a car or take the train to work, since you probably know the price of a train ticket.

We will return to the car analogy when we get to the maths; I think that the best practical definition of LCOE is 'what would you have to pay someone per MWh to build the power plant and sell electricity to you?' In fact, if you are a government or electricity market planner, the easiest way to find out is to hold an auction — declare that you plan to buy, say, 5,000 GWh at the lowest price bid. Then let the companies which specialise in developing solar projects figure out what they want to offer; there is now enough competition that you will get multiple bids and there will be pressure on bidders to submit their lowest price.

If you want to duplicate a bidder's process with your own model, there are three major variables (and one minor one, which is the operation and maintenance cost — see Chapter 19). The first is the 'capital expenditure' (capex) of the solar project, the cost per W, which we have already discussed. The second is how sunny it is at the location (i.e. the insolation, but there is really no advantage to using a technical term here. And many spellcheckers 'correct' it to insulation). Sunniness can be measured, but not controlled, and determines the 'capacity factor', which is how much energy is generated per year, usually expressed as a percentage equivalent to the hours running at full capacity. Naturally, a solar project generates more energy in a sunny place than in a less sunny place — the capacity factor of a rooftop photovoltaic system in Germany is likely to be 10–13%, in southern California 16–21%.

The third, and conceptually most difficult for those of us raised by science teachers, is the cost of capital and time value of money. This will require a short diversion through the history and ethics of lending at interest. It also applies to the car analogy, where you may have to borrow money at interest to buy a car, or at least will need to tie up your savings in the car; see Table 14.1.

Would you rather have $100 today, or $100 in a year's time? Probably, the answer is easy; even if there is nothing you want to buy, you could put the money in a bank account today and earn at least a pittance — let's say 1%/year — of interest, so that you would have $101 in a year's time. For such a small return, you might simply decide to spend it on beer, or put it

Table 14.1.   Analogy: Levelised cost of energy of a power plant versus cost of running a car per mile.

| Component of LCOE | Equivalent component of cost per kilometre | Notes |
|---|---|---|
| Capital expenditure (capex) to setup project | Cost of buying car | For a renewable energy project, this is most of the total cost. |
| Capacity factor | Kilometres driven per year | For a renewable energy project, this depends on the resource. For a gas-fired power plant it depends on how much the plant is needed. |
| Fixed costs/ operation and maintenance cost | Cost of insurance and service | This is less important the more energy generated or distance driven. It is also historically very low for solar projects, but see Chapter 19. |
| Variable costs, e.g. fuel | Fuel cost | Zero for a solar or wind plant. Considerable for a fossil fuel plant. Can be negative for a plant burning rubbish which needs to be disposed of. |
| Cost of capital | Interest on auto loan for purchase (or opportunity cost of spending your savings on a car) | This is more important for renewable energy plants than for fossil fuel plants, because more of the cost is upfront. It is also a more important factor in high-risk countries where interest rates and cost of equity are high. |

towards a really good-quality item of clothing which you'd enjoy wearing all year. This is how low interest rates stimulate consumer spending.

Would you rather have $102 in a year's time, or $100 now? What about $110 in a year? These answers really depend on you, both your rational and your irrational decision-making. If you have credit card debt on which you pay interest of 15%/year, rationally you should pick the $100 now unless offered more than $115 next year. But you might be offered $120 in a year, and yet really really want that $100 now as you are about to go on holiday and want spending money. Whatever you feel, the money has a time value to you, and you have an implied personal 'hurdle rate' determined by the opportunity cost of other investments; 1% if you cannot think of anything better to do than put it in the bank, 15% if you could use it to pay some of the credit card debt, perhaps more if having that $100 to spend on holiday means a lot to you.

The other thing that affects your decision is the risk. In the example above, we have assumed that you trust the person offering you money now or more money in a year. What if you don't? If you think the person is totally flaky, you'll take $100 now instead of any amount of money in a year. If you expect that they pay up but have some doubts, you might increase your hurdle rate/cost of equity (the two terms mean essentially the same thing).

Businesses and financiers are generally more rational in their financial decision-making than individuals, and so their hurdle rates are usually determined by other uses of cash available to them ('opportunity cost'), with consideration for the risk of investments. Taking higher risk should always require a higher return, as a basic principle of finance. This is one reason why banks set credit card interest rates higher than mortgage interest rates; if the mortgage owner cannot pay the interest, the bank gets the house and can sell it, while if a credit card owner does not pay, the bank may never get any of the money back (car loans are somewhere in the middle, as a car can be resold but for much less than its original price, and car loans may also be cross-subsidised by car manufacturers to increase sales).

The anarchist historian David Graeber points out in his entertaining book *Debt: the First 5,000 Years* (2014) that "looking over world literature, it is impossible to find a single sympathetic representative of a moneylender, or anyway a professional moneylender, which means by definition one who charges interest". He has a point there, but there's an argument that debt is not a bad thing.

Imagine a world with no debt. It's not that difficult — for much of European history, the practice of usury has been outlawed or severely controlled by the state. Jewish people, who were often banned from other businesses, were the main providers of consumer debt and were periodically persecuted for it even by the people who used their services. In much of the developing world, the network of banks offering debt to individuals still doesn't exist as of 2018. On the plus side, this means no pushy advertisements of payday loans for beer and holidays at exorbitant rates of interest (which people are free to take or leave, but can be cynically targeted to exploit the financially illiterate). On the minus side, it means poor people have no access to capital when they could use it profitably. A small-time vegetable grower cannot borrow money to buy a handcart which would quadruple the amount she can sell every time she walks to the market, and pay off its initial investment in months. A farmer can't buy an irrigation pump that would triple the production of his fields and save him hours of backbreaking labour every day.

Sometime in the 20th century, Western banks realised that their previous policy of lending money only to kings who can levy taxes or rich gentlepersons with land assets was causing them to miss out on profits from lending to higher-risk people at higher rates of interest. "If you never miss a plane, you spend too much time in airports" pointed out Nobel Prize-winning economist George Stigler — in other words, if you lend money to many people and never have one not pay you, you are being unduly cautious. There are probably many slightly more risky prospective borrowers, who could reasonably pay a higher rate of interest, more than enough to justify the occasional failure to pay back.

An extreme example of this is microfinance, which is regarded as a powerful tool for reducing poverty in developing countries, even though interest rates can be over 25%. They are not necessarily the answer to everything — a study on microloans [Banerjee *et al.*, 2015], noted 'a consistent pattern of modestly positive, but not transformative, effects'. However, microfinance may be more appropriate for renewable energy than for other types of loans. This will be discussed further in Chapter 21.

The cost of capital is much more important when determining the cost of renewable energy than for gas, coal or diesel, because nearly all the renewable energy cost is upfront, and interest payments (or dividends to equity holders) are a major part of the plant's lifetime expenses. The higher the cost of capital, the higher the levelised cost of energy generation. In general, the cost of capital is split into two parts (sometimes more): debt and equity. The equity holder is the legal owner of the project, just like a homeowner, while the debt provider has lent them the money to buy the project, like a mortgage provider on a house.

The interest rate on the debt is likely to be lower than the cost of equity, because the debt holder carries less risk: if the project produces less revenue than expected, the debt investor gets paid their interest anyway, while the equity holder suffers. Only once the project is performing so badly that the equity owner is getting nothing does the debt holder suffer — and since the project will usually be funded with about 10–30% equity, that is some serious underperformance. For solar and wind projects, debt is usually 'non-recourse', i.e. the debt investor/bank cannot ask the owner to reach into their other assets and compensate them if the project goes horribly wrong and does not produce enough cash to pay the interest on the debt. The equity owner expects a higher rate of return from their money than the interest rate, because they take more risk, but will also get any 'upside' if the project performs better than expected. Borrowing debt increases the return on equity investment by 'leveraging' it, and in fact affects the weighted average cost of capital by more than that, because interest payments are tax-deductible expenses. All-equity large solar projects are very unusual, although all-equity funding is common in household solar systems in Europe, where individual people (i.e. not corporations) often have limited options for investing their money.

The LCOE is a function of all those things — capex, resource, and cost of capital (and operating costs, like maintenance). It's really something you backcalculate from modelling the returns on a system where a power price (or annual revenue or savings, power price times generation) is an input.

Let's create a very simple discounted cash flow model, where a household solar system costing $5,000 saves the owner $300/year, and the owner is satisfied with a return of 5% (her bank is offering her 2%/year interest, and although she considers the bank safer, she also likes the idea of being green and independent from her utility). For simplicity, let's assume she installs it at the very beginning of year 1, and that maintenance consists of a routine system check-up and clean every 2 years, costing $100 (see Table 14.2).

The discounted cashflow is a way to make sense of the line 'total cashflow in year' taking into account the time value of money. By dividing the cashflow in a given year by the discount factor in the fourth line — with 5% the interest rate — you equate the value of a series of cashflows

Table 14.2.   Cashflows for the first 8 years of a residential PV system.

| | Year 1 | Year 2 | Year 3 | Year 4 | Year 5 | Year 6 | Year 7 | Year 8 |
|---|---|---|---|---|---|---|---|---|
| Initial cost | −$5,000 | | | | | | | |
| Maintenance cost | | | −$100 | | −$100 | | −$100 | |
| Annual savings (power price * generation) | $300 | $300 | $300 | $300 | $300 | $300 | $300 | $300 |
| Total cashflow in year | −$4,700 | $300 | $200 | $300 | $200 | $300 | $200 | $300 |
| Discount factor | 0 | $1/(1+5\%)$ | $1/(1+5\%)^2$ | $1/(1+5\%)^3$ | $1/(1+5\%)^4$ | $1/(1+5\%)^5$ | $1/(1+5\%)^6$ | $1/(1+5\%)^7$ |
| Discounted cashflow at 5% (i.e. cashflow times discount factor) | −$4,700 | $286 | $181 | $259 | $165 | $235 | $149 | $213 |

in the future with a lump sum in the present. So $285.7 today would be worth $300 next year to you, if your cost of capital is 5%. You can sum these, and if the sum of the discounted cashflows is positive and you trust all your inputs, you should make the investment.

We can easily figure out that the initial investment pays back in year 20, but our plant owner is savvy and wants a return of 5%, so is this solar system a good deal for her over 25 years? This is much easier to do in Microsoft Excel or similar software, and I recommend that you do this if you are seriously interested in the topic. I calculate that this is a very bad investment, with a 'net present value' of minus $1,234. If she drops her return requirement to 2%, however (maybe she gets extremely annoyed with her utility), this is achievable.

Levelised Cost of Energy is simply the power price the owner gets (or saves) for each MWh, to make the project worth doing (a net present value of zero or higher). This is usually stated assuming that the power price paid, and the maintenance cost, rises with inflation.

Of course, a real project finance model is massively more complex than this — it will include cashflows to equity, cashflows to debt (which can be set up in different ways), tax, may handle cashflows seasonally or monthly rather than just annually, and may have changing revenues (the power price may rise over time, or of course it may fall). Engineering a project for the maximum financial value is an art and a science. But the basic principle is sound, and may be helpful in everyday life if you are trying to decide on a present investment with future payoff (as in the car vs bus ticket analogy — you can include all kinds of extra cashflows such as the ability to make non-commute trips with a car).

To summarise, levelised cost of energy is a function of the initial capital expenditure to build the project, the cost of capital and the resource (and to a lesser extent, the maintenance costs). If someone tells you a LCOE for a renewable energy project without including at least these three variables, they probably don't properly understand the under-lying calculation and may have used very incorrect assumptions. The most common among academics is to assume that money is free, which will be a shock when they apply for a mortgage. The most common among people selling solar systems is to assume electricity prices will rise strongly and continuously over the entire 25 years, which cuts the level they need to start at, and boosts the internal rate of return of the project substantially. The problem with assuming this is that it may not actually happen; electricity prices can fall as well as rise, particularly over 25-year periods.

## 14.2. Cost of Capital and the Role of Development Banks

Governments and multinational organisations often seek to reduce the cost or LCOE of renewables. They cannot influence the capacity factor or, in the short term, the capex (they can make long-term strategic investment in research and development, which might yield innovations to reduce capex. The US government's Sunshot programme tries to do this by providing research grants and studies).

The main lever that governments can pull to support renewable energy is to reduce the cost of capital, either by reducing the risk of a project or by setting up as an investor themselves. Providing a guaranteed power price for all production, through a feed-in tariff or an individually negotiated power price, is a way to reduce 'offtake risk', the risk that the project will be unable to sell its power at a required price.

Other governments support renewables through a development bank, a way to support infrastructure investment they consider desirable. Many development banks were founded after a specific period of disruption, to help rebuild and promote peace and prosperity. They have become extremely important to renewable energy deployment; in 2016, eight development banks invested $55 billion in clean energy and renewables [Gombar, 2017], compared with BNEF's estimate of $324.6 billion invested in renewables in that year (although the methodologies and sectors covered are a little different for the two figures). While $55 billion was the direct investment, most development banks aim to bring in much more capital from private sector investors by acting as the first taker of risk ('leveraging') or by providing guidance and information. For example, the International Finance Corporation (the part of the World Bank Group most involved in bringing in private investment) calculates that 'since 1956, IFC has leveraged $2.6 billion in capital to deliver more than $265 billion in financing for businesses in developing countries' [IFC website, July 2018].

The German Kreditbank für Wiederaufbau (KfW), the Credit Bank for Reconstruction, was founded in 1948 to repair houses damaged in the Second World War and to rebuild the country's energy system, and now supports student loans, individual investments, municipalities and small businesses in Germany as well as environmental infrastructure and exports by German companies abroad. KfW assisted the German solar boom by providing loans to local German banks, which then provided low-interest loans to small firms and individuals for rooftop solar. This allowed them to benefit from feed-in tariffs without having to spend much (if any) money upfront. In 2016, KfW was the most active development bank in renewable energy and energy efficiency worldwide, investing $34 billion or nearly 40% of its total deployment in these sectors [Gombar, 2017].

Another post-Second World War creation, the World Bank Group, was founded as the International Bank for Reconstruction and Development in 1944. It is now a group of five institutions with 189 member countries and a remit to end poverty and promote prosperity in developing countries.

The European Bank for Reconstruction and Development (EBRD) was set up 'in haste' (according to its website) in 1991, to respond to the collapse of communism in former Soviet Bloc countries. It now also invests in Mongolia, Turkey, Greece and northern African countries, and, unusually, requires that member countries be democratic.

Other development banks have more specific national priorities. Brazil founded its own development bank, BNDES, in 1952 to invest in industry and infrastructure in the country. The China Development Bank was founded in 1994, with a remit to "serve China's major long-term economic and social development strategies," and claims plausibly in 2018 to be the world's largest development bank. The African Development Bank Group was founded in 1964 by 23 African countries to promote sustainable economic growth and reduce poverty on their continent, and later grew to include all African countries (according to the bank's website as of July 2018) and 26 non-African member countries.

Morgan Bazilian, former Lead Energy Specialist at the World Bank, now Research Professor of Public Policy at the Colorado School of Mines, notes that renewable energy is an increasing part of development banks' work. "Renewable energy is dramatically increasing as a percentage of development portfolios both because of cost declines and because of demand from client countries."

One principle of development banks is that they should not replace ('crowd out') private sector investment. If government and development funding is too easily and widely available, it can reduce the opportunities for private investors to make good deals, and prevent the emergence of a healthy financial ecosystem. Consequently, most development banks are trying to fund or support only projects that would not happen without their help.

According to Morgan Bazilian, this balance is becoming increasingly complex. "As prices have declined dramatically, and an appetite from private investors to participate in emerging market has increased, development banks have more difficulty finding a role that does not compete directly with private finance. Their role is thus shifting towards advising on the design of regulatory frameworks and policy formation, and providing various risk mitigation tools, and also focusing on those countries in desperate need of help" ('fragile and conflict states' in development bank terminology).

In January 2015, the World Bank's International Finance Corporation launched a programme called Scaling Solar, which provides a package of services to help countries (especially developing ones) get privately funded solar projects within 2 years. Scaling Solar includes a standardised tendering/auction process with competitive financing, guarantees and insurance available to all bidders, templates for project documents, and advice on project siting and grid integration. This last is important, as there is no point building a solar project if you cannot get the energy onto the grid. An early 8.5 MW project built in Rwanda, by Norwegian firm Scatec Solar, was initially hit by rolling blackouts which took the grid down for 25% of the time and made the project unable to export its generation during these hours.

Scaling Solar aimed to break the deadlock that many developing countries found themselves in after 2010. Several countries, including Jordan, Kenya, Nigeria and Egypt, had discussed power contracts to solar projects and even agreed prices, but the whole process took so long that before the projects were built, the prices looked extremely overgenerous and the governments balked and found reasons to back out and renegotiate.

Zambia was the first country to sign a mandate with the Scaling Solar programme, in August 2016, followed by Senegal, Madagascar and Ethiopia. The programme has not entirely succeeded in its aim of deploying solar in 2 years; the first project in Zambia is expected to be built in September 2018, over 3 years after the country signed up. It has also been criticised for a cookie-cutter approach which fails to involve local conditions, and for a blind focus on costs (to be fair, these are part of the point of the programme).

It has certainly achieved the aim of low costs; the planned projects in Zambia will be paid $60.2/MWh and $78.4/MWh, fixed in US dollars (i.e. investors are protected from a weakening in the Zambian currency, the kwacha) for 25 years. This is partly possible because of the guaranteed financing. BNEF estimated in June 2016 that the cost of debt to Zambia's Scaling Solar projects was about 6%, compared with 10–12% for other Zambia bonds paid in US dollars without development bank involvement. The second Scaling Solar project to go to auction, in Senegal, was won with even lower bids of 38–40 euros ($44–47)/MWh in April 2018. This is, by any reasonable standard, cheap energy for countries which need it.

# Chapter 15

# 2014 and 2015: Solar Auctions, Auto-Consumption and Sun Taxes

The solar market started to look brighter for some firms in 2014. Prices stabilised across the value chain, long-term polysilicon contracts expired and the best module manufacturers started to make positive profit margins. The European feed-in tariff policies had generally been removed or brought under control, and the solar markets of Western Europe contracted, installing an approximately flat amount year-on-year after the spectacular booms and busts of 2004–2011.

## 15.1. Big Solar

Meanwhile, the governments of China and Japan became serious about solar, in very different ways. The Chinese government had tried to support its solar manufacturers in the previous 5 years through cheap land and cheap debt, but really threw its weight behind incentives for new build in 2014. It allocated a feed-in tariff and then quotas of projects by province, most of which were built on schedule. Some of the sunny, sparsely populated Chinese provinces, such as Gansu and Qinghai in the northwest of the huge country, had difficulty transporting the power to the cities, and did not need it locally. China's National Energy Administration estimates that 31% of solar and 39% of wind generated electricity in Gansu had to be 'curtailed' (curtailment is when electricity is thrown away because the capacity to transport it did not exist) in 2015, and this worsened in 2016. The country now plans new transmission lines to reduce this problem both for solar and wind, and a more rational way of deciding which plants run. Due to the way the Chinese power market is planned, with fixed prices by technology rather than a power market, it is sometimes advisable to curtail a renewable energy project and run a coal plant instead — which clearly makes no sense. The government is also taking measures to encourage developers to build solar plants in the east of China, which is less sunny than the northwest, but has many more cities that need the power. These measures are already working; the national solar curtailment rate in China fell to 5.8% in 2017, from 10.1% in 2016, with solar and wind together generating 6.72% of the country's electricity (PV contributing 1.75%), according to China's National Energy Administration.

Japan introduced a European-style feed-in tariff in 2012, and repeated the mistake of setting the level of tariff at about the level that the domestic solar industry asked for. The country also made the tariff applicable to projects when they applied for the tariff, not when they got built — so you could apply, and then wait several years for equipment costs to drop before spending the money on building. In addition, the application for the tariff was initially such an easy process that many companies submitted applications to the Japanese Ministry of Energy, Trade and Investment (METI) before they had even established rights to the land, never mind planning permission. The result was an expensive, slow boom, modulated constantly by METI tweaking the rules. The boom is running out of steam as of 2018 because the regulator has allowed utilities to limit how much can be installed in their service area, but in 2014 and 2015 Japan was the world's second largest PV market after China.

Europe had enough solar, and most countries were on track to build or had already built as much as they had put into their National Renewable Energy Action Plans. Since the Germans started uncapped feed-in tariffs in 2004, successive governments implemented them and caused a boom and bust in large-scale ground-mounted projects; the last one was the UK, where the government had never really meant to encourage large solar at all. Roof-mounted PV is generally viewed favourably by politicians as it means votes, but it is very difficult to set prices to encourage only roof-top solar. By the end of 2015, Germany had entirely eliminated feed-in tariffs for projects over 500 kW, and tariffs for smaller systems were lower than the power prices paid by businesses and households.

A new idea started to take hold; instead of trying to calculate the prices you had to pay companies to build solar, why not turn it around and ask for the lowest price companies would build solar for? From a government's perspective this is very attractive. A competitive auction should get the best price for power without the government having to calculate it themselves and inevitably get it wrong, plus the government can control exactly how much gets built. Latin American countries, South Africa, the United Arab Emirates and India were some of the first and most enthusiastic countries to adopt tenders, but France and Germany followed suit. For the French, the criteria are complex and opaque, and this may be intended to benefit French companies at the expense of foreign ones without explicitly contravening European free trade laws. Apparently out of curiosity, the German government held several competitive tenders for very large solar, and received prices around 82–85 euros/MWh in 2015 — setting a new benchmark low for the country (in 2018, these fell below 50 euros/MWh).

The auctions generally worked well, with new record lows for the price of solar power being set every few months from 2015 to 2017. The first Dubai tender was won at below $60/MWh in late 2014 due to a combination of competitive capex, great sun and relatively low-cost debt from Saudi banks. In 2015, the UK held its first (and as of 2018, only) solar auction. It is called Contract for Difference, because governments love coming up with new names for things made out of words for other things. Major developer Lightsource bid at 79.23 UK pounds/MWh, escalated annually with inflation. This compares with 92 pounds/MWh, also rising with inflation, for nuclear plant Hinkley Point agreed at roughly the same time. It started to seem unreasonable to say that solar was simply too expensive.

Of course auctions bring their own problems. One of these is that if the barrier to bidding in the auction is low — which governments want, to ensure that the auction is a competition between many players — it can attract rather speculative bids from companies hoping to win a contract at any price. These companies' plan is to hope for a stroke of good luck, like a collapse in technology price or cost of debt, which allows them to build the project at a profit. Some simply seem to have misunderstood the auction rules. For example, in the UK's Contract for Difference auction, you get what you bid. One inexperienced developer bid 50 pounds/MWh, a price that was clearly impossible, apparently expecting to be paid the highest winning price; they promptly admitted on LinkedIn that this was not feasible and withdrew from the auction. Some early Indian solar thermal projects have not been built, presumably because the prices were not rational. Some of the Brazilian projects bid will not be built, mainly because a fall in the value of the Brazilian reais makes them economically unattractive.

Strictly speaking, it is not a big problem for a government if companies win an auction and then can't deliver. It wastes the time of everyone involved, but PV is quick to build, after all, they can always run another auction and hope the bidders take it more seriously this time. This can be partially enforced by requiring bidders to 'post a bid bond' (pay money into a government account, which they will get back if they deliver their project but lose if they screw up) to get a power contract, or by requiring bidders to have a minimum of previous experience. Unfortunately, some governments, particularly in Latin America, the Middle East and Africa, have felt embarrassed by having selected a bidder who cannot deliver, and go to irrational lengths to avoid this (such as finding another company to buy the winning bidder, and build the project, in exchange for a later more favourable contract). In general, embarrassment is a poor reason for abandoning the principles of capitalism in the middle of a fundamentally capitalist process.

## 15.2.  Small Solar

In the first quarter of 2012, the German feed-in tariff for solar plants below 10 kW dropped below the average power price paid by households, as part of the scheduled reductions in the feed-in tariff. For the first time, German households began to care when they generated solar electricity and when they used it, because they saved more money by using it directly than they would get from the grid.

The results were not dramatic, as batteries are still much too expensive to build for such a small gain (though a battery subsidy starting in 2013 drove several thousand systems), but there were small shifts.

For example, installers began to put up systems facing slightly west, so that they lost power in the morning but generated more in the evening when the homeowner was home to use it.

In late 2014, Germany passed a law to raise more funding for its EEG subsidy fund, this time from solar projects. The owners of new PV projects over 10 kW (i.e. not household systems) paid a surcharge for solar power they used instead of buying from the grid. This was only 2–3 euro-cents/kWh (it increased slightly in 2016 and 2017) and could be argued to cover some of the costs of the distribution grid. The projects also get a feed-in tariff for exported energy, which while not as high as the avoided cost of buying power, is better than nothing.

Germans continue to build solar, although the frenetic boom was over and the tariff (now paid only for exports) comes down further if it begins again. The German tariff is now linked to build volumes, with annual new build over 2.5 GW under the feed-in tariff resulting in a decline of the tariff. In 2018, volumes edged over the 2.5 GW limit and the feed-in tariff fell slightly. Since new solar projects get paid much less, the cost of wholesale power has risen, and thanks to the self-consumption tax, the surcharge on power bills in Germany to pay for renewables fell a little in 2018, and will be 6.405 euro-cents/kWh consumed in 2019.

In sunny Spain in December 2014, the government realised that homeowners could save money by putting up a solar rooftop, without any subsidy at all or even net metering (where solar generation runs the meter backwards). This represented a potential threat to Spain's existing power generators, and to the entire power sector if a lot of consumers stopped buying in the daytime. The government brought in a 'sun tax' of about 5 euro-cents/kWh self-consumed, with no export payment for selling to the grid. There was more public outrage about this than the German sun tax, possibly because it directly affects homeowners rather than corporations, and also because it is more economically punitive.

Italy also had solar cheaper than the grid. In 2014, the country brought in a new version of net metering, where exports to the grid are paid at the wholesale rate for power (about 50–70 euros/MWh, versus 250–300 euros/MWh paid by households for electricity, plus projects are exempt from grid fees amounting to about another 50–70 euros/MWh).

Many US states have had net metering for years, but it mostly didn't matter because solar was too expensive. There were caps to net metering, but they were far from being met. In 2014 and 2015, utilities started lobbying more forcefully to cut net metering laws, increased fixed charges to solar owners for being connected to the grid, and change net metering to a lower export tariff (as in effect has happened in Italy and Germany).

A number of US firms founded to build and arrange financing for solar on rooftops continued to grow strongly in 2014 and 2015. SolarCity, Sunrun and Vivint Solar became industry names, aiming to become household names with public marketing campaigns and large sales forces.

The age of rooftop solar competitive with the grid had begun.

# Chapter 16

# 2016–2018: Solar Is Cheap, but What Does It Mean?

After 2015, it became increasingly undeniable that large-scale photovoltaics is the cheapest way of generating electricity in some countries. This shifts the focus of solar policy away from bulk subsidies for generation, towards more tailored incentives attempting to get the best prices and to match electricity generation to demand. We are living in the early days of cheap photovoltaics.

## 16.1. More Low Solar Bids in Auctions

Dubai's second photovoltaic tender awarded 800 MW at a price of $29.9/MWh in June 2016, a new record. In August 2016, Chile beat this, with $29.1/MWh. In December 2017, a Mexican auction had an average solar price bid of $20.8/MWh (all these projects are to be built several years after they were bid). As you might expect from the levelised cost of energy calculation, sunny countries with relatively good political stability tend to attract lower bids; the cost of financing is low and the output high. Below $30/MWh is definitely in a range competitive with natural gas; the US Energy Information Administration's *Annual Energy Outlook 2018* pegs the cost of new combined cycle gas plants in 2022 at $48.3/MWh, of which $32.8/MWh is variable costs.

The auctions became more complex as the numbers dropped. Abu Dhabi's first solar tender, in September 2016, asked developers to bid to cover a particular patch of land with solar panels, while paying 1.6 times as much for power in the months from June to September as in the rest of the year. The idea of this was to match output to power demand, which in Abu Dhabi peaks in the hottest months due to air conditioning use. The winning bid was to supply power at a price averaging around $29.4/MWh. These prices were seldom transparent about their inflation assumptions, which make a big difference to the headline figure; a price of $29 rising at 3%/year is almost certainly better than $30 fixed.

In Chile, the government took another approach and ran a technology-agnostic auction, where developers bid to supply electricity within particular periods of the day, regardless of what type of generation. Since parts of Chile are extremely sunny, PV projects won the daytime blocks, at a lower price ($29.1/MWh) than the gas which won the base-load contracts.

## 16.2. The Battle for US Rooftops

In the US, the main federal support for solar was (and is until 2021) an Investment Tax Credit (ITC), which allows solar investors to claim back 30% of their investment against the taxes payable for this year. This is quite generous, but the catch is that you need to be paying enough tax to fully benefit from this tax credit. For a normal household, this may not be the case; therefore a substantial industry grew up offering 'third-party solar financing' where a company like SolarCity (now a division of Tesla), Vivint or SunRun would arrange for an investor to own solar systems on residential roofs. The residents of the house sign a 20 or 25-year agreement to buy the power at a favourable price compared with grid electricity. This was assisted by a second subsidy in many states, 'net metering', which essentially ran a consumer's meter backwards any time their solar system was producing more than the house was consuming. SolarCity/SunRun/Vivint would collect investment from firms which pay a lot of tax — investment banks like Morgan Stanley or JPMorgan, for example — and manage a large number of residential rooftops and their power payments.

There is nothing particularly wrong with this business model. It's not necessarily efficient from a subsidy-minimising perspective, because companies tend to report the cost of the system as rather more than it needed to be, in order to claim higher tax credit. However, everyone involved in the deal can get what they want. SolarCity and SunRun were hot venture capital investments which achieved profitable exits by listing on US stock markets in 2015, raising money and their profile.

US companies are seldom content to stay small, and venture funded companies need to be ambitious to please their investors. However, it did not seem likely that the opportunity would last forever. Throughout 2014 and 2015, the ITC was scheduled to expire at the end of 2015 and there was a rush to build portfolios of projects while it was possible; a surprise extension of the ITC into 2016, to continue at its current rate to the end of 2019, was an anticlimax. SolarCity, in particular, spent a lot of money on sales and marketing (until the second quarter of 2016, its sales and marketing expenses were consistently more than its revenues), aiming to get a huge number of rooftops under management and become a household name.

However, the consumer case for third-party financing has been growing weaker. The cost of a new rooftop solar system has fallen, even in America, where the structure of the ITC encouraged high prices. This made the initial cost look more manageable to households and increased the probability that they could write the tax credit off against their own income tax. In addition, locking yourself in to a 20 or 25-year power purchase agreement at a fixed rate, or one which rose with inflation, was looking less a no-brainer even if the initial rate was lower than you were currently paying. In consequence, more households started to simply borrow the money to install the solar system, on the basis that then they get all the benefit once the system was paid off. The proportion of US residential solar systems built using third-party financing dropped to 30% in Q3 2017, from more than 48% throughout 2015 and 2016.

Along with other factors, such as the bankruptcy of SunEdison and the continued losses of these companies, this made 2016 a bad year for the stock prices of residential installation companies. SunRun's stock price fell 55% over the year, Vivint Solar's 10%. SolarCity's stock price fell 59% from the start of 2016 until it was bought out in November by Tesla, the electric vehicle company founded by entrepreneur and visionary Elon Musk and engineers JB Straubel and Martin Eberhard in 2003. Tesla has essentially put its financial strength behind the struggling SolarCity. Whether this will pay off remains to be seen.

In May 2018, California is trying a new approach to increasing the uptake of solar at a low cost. The state had 11.8% of its generation from solar already in 2017, according to US Energy Information Administration data. It has passed an amendment to building codes, requiring that newly built homes under three stories high install enough PV to net out the annual kWh used by the house. There are some exemptions which apply to, for example, very shaded places. This simultaneously encourages the houses to be constructed to be energy-efficient, and ensures that solar panels will be installed at the best time to do so — when the roof is being put up, and workers are on the roof anyway. It means that the solar systems will not need separate scaffolding (which can cost about 10% of a solar system price), can be designed with the house, and can be put up in relatively large numbers at once, reducing the cost to drive between the sites. These costs are actually significant, as team efficiency shoots up when members are trained and experienced enough to complete a system in a single day. California's is not the world's first rooftop solar mandate, but it is the largest, and probably well-timed to deliver a lot of quite cheap solar.

In September 2018, the state passed a bill, SB100, setting a target of 100% of its generation from zero-carbon sources (including nuclear and potentially fossil fuels with carbon capture) by 2045. Interim targets are 50% renewables (excluding nuclear) by 2026 and 60% renewables by 2030. Since California, if it was a country, would be the world's fifth largest economy in 2017, this is a lot of renewables and other zero carbon electricity.

## 16.3. China Slams on the Brakes

China's PV companies installed a record 53 GW in the country in 2017, nearly half the world build. We knew this was unsustainable, as the country pays subsidies out of a surcharge on power prices which feeds the Renewable Energy Fund. As of mid-2018, this was in deficit by $19 billion, and the Ministry of Finance is unwilling to increase the surcharge on power bills and free up more capital.

In theory, China's new PV build was controlled by a system of quotas for receiving the subsidy (mostly feed-in tariffs) handed out by the federal government to provinces. The problem was that developers often build projects before they had been allocated subsidy, on the assumption that they would be first in line for next year's. In consequence, despite the quota system, the spending was out of control.

On June 1, 2018, China's policymakers slammed on the brakes, freezing the issue of new quota to subsidise photovoltaics. In principle, solar may not need subsidies in China, as the levelised cost of electricity is lower than the government-set power price, based on the cost of fossil generation, in several provinces. However, the country is trying to liberalise its power market (i.e. make it an actual market with prices set by costs), which brings uncertainty and may result in lower prices in future. We expect more moderate build in China in future, and the sudden halt of support is likely to hurt solar manufacturers in 2019 with an oversupply of components.

A coda to this is that 7 GW of projects, a quantity comparable to the entire annual market in the US or in Europe, missed the Chinese deadline of June 30 and commissioned in July 2018. Sometimes you can slam on the brakes but the car keeps sliding. As of late 2018, the Chinese government is discussing how it can find money to build more solar.

## 16.4. The World in Solar in Late 2018

Torn between the desire to meet climate targets and please the public, and fear of disruptive change to the energy system, governments are trying

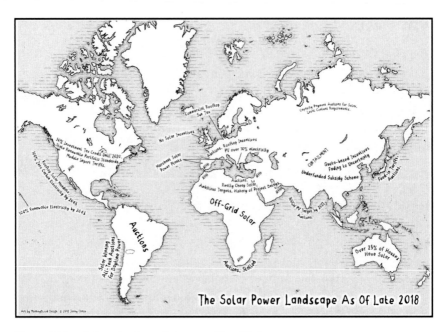

Figure 16.1.   Selected solar policies, as of late 2018.

*Source*: Art by Glynn Seal of MonkeyBlood Design.

various incentives or disincentives for solar. Rooftop mandates, auctions, and export tariffs to support rooftop solar — plus both sun taxes and fixed fees for being connected to the grid — are in play around the world.

What is clear today is that solar is nearly everywhere (Figure 16.1) and not going away.

# Chapter 17

# Technology Focus: Solar Thermal Electricity Generation

Chapter 10 detailed how, in a normal power market, simultaneous power supply, demand and the cost of generating a marginal MWh sets the price of power. Generally in hot countries, peak power demand is in the daytime for air conditioning, but continues well into the late afternoon and into evening when the outside temperature is still high and people come home to cook dinner. This load is not well served by photovoltaics, the output of which drops sharply in the late afternoon as the sun gets low.

One option for supplying the evening peak in electricity demand in a grid with plenty of photovoltaics is solar thermal electricity generation. This is also called concentrated solar power, CSP, though I dislike this term as there is also a concentrated form of PV. Concentrated PV doesn't work very well and has largely been abandoned as a commercial option, but it is a technology.

Solar thermal electricity generation sounds good in principle. It uses a turbine, which can turn in time with the grid frequency and hence stabilise the grid. The heat can be stored during the daytime in tanks of molten salt or blocks of stone, and used to run the plant after the sun goes down, potentially for the whole 24 h, or just for the 4–6 h required for people to cook dinner and watch TV after sundown. Natural gas can be used to boost the capacity utilisation of the turbine, which may offend purists, but is a whole lot better than just having a gas plant. Solar thermal is a favourite new technology of the International Energy Agency in its forecasts, perhaps because it continues to look like a familiar fossil fuel plant in many important technical respects.

The history of commercial solar thermal starts with the Luz or SEGS plants in California's Mojave desert, developed between 1985 and 1990 by Israeli firm Luz (which means 'light' in Hebrew — back then it was much more forgivable to have no imagination with solar company names). These were parabolic trough designs, and generally worked to specifications. Unfortunately, Luz overstretched itself financially when a key tax credit was not renewed, and went bankrupt in 1991 (noting, probably accurately, that at the time it produced 90% of the world's solar power). The 350 MW of SEGS parabolic trough solar thermal plants were sold for less than it cost to build them. They are still operating today after several changes of ownership.

The SEGS financial disaster, which does not appear to have been a technology problem, cooled enthusiasm for solar thermal for several decades until Spain experimented with a solar thermal subsidy in 2007. Over the next 5 years Spanish companies built 2.3 GW of plants, nearly all parabolic trough. The consensus began to build, however, that the only way to significantly reduce cost was to move to tower designs.

Fundamentally, solar thermal towers (Figure 17.1) sound compelling. Parabolic troughs (pictured in Figure 2.2 back in Chapter 2) have literally kilometres of 'receiver tubes' carrying hot fluid, which need to be positioned above the mirrors and turn with the mirror to catch the sun. The temperature is limited to about 400°C and it is relatively difficult to use a better heat transfer fluid like molten salt instead of steam.

Towers, by contrast, have a single focal point and thousands of mirrors ('heliostats') mounted on the ground, tilting to focus the sunlight on the elevated tower. This needs to be a work of perfect coordination, but the resulting hot fluid does not need to travel so far to reach the turbine, and temperatures up to 580°C are possible. This is useful as the higher the temperature, the more efficiently a steam turbine can run and the more energy can be stored in a given volume of molten salt. Solar thermal engineers generally love towers as they are a very elegant solution compared with miles of tubing, and can get to higher temperatures, achieving a better efficiency. This is because the higher the temperature difference between two sources, the better the efficiency of an engine

Figure 17.1.   The Ivanpah tower and heliostat solar thermal project.
*Source*: Shutterstock.

running on this difference. The maximum possible is called the Carnot efficiency.

There are several other designs of solar thermal plant, notably Fresnel concentrators and parabolic dish systems, but they appear to be dying out (see Figure 17.2). Most of the world's 5.2 GW of installed solar thermal capacity is parabolic trough, with 685 MW of towers commissioned worldwide and several more GW in the planning stage (as of late 2018).

Solar thermal is one of the obvious solutions to the problem of evening peak demand in sunny countries, and like PV, costs have come down somewhat and the companies involved say it has much further to fall. However, in practice it seems to combine many of the engineering challenges of running a fossil fuel or nuclear plant with those of collecting a distributed resource. There are pipes to explode, moving parts to wear, and in the case of plants with molten salt storage, the additional fun that molten salt freezes under about 240°C, so the pipes become full of solid salt. Molten salt sometimes leaks out. And you cannot control the input heat as you can

Figure 17.2.   A Fresnel concentrator solar thermal design. The advantage of this is that the mirrors are simple flat ones and the receiver tubes are above the mirrors and stationary (unlike with parabolic trough where the receiver tubes must tilt with the troughs, requiring complex joints). The disadvantage is that high temperatures are difficult to reach.
*Source*: Shutterstock.

in a fossil plant — factors like the amount of dust in the upper atmosphere, which is hard to detect from satellite data, seem to have a bigger impact on performance than for PV because of nonlinearities (solar thermal plants get less efficient as the temperature they can reach drops).

The solar thermal industry has (in my opinion) more than its share of poor performing plants, particularly towers, and very few it can cite as technical successes. Data released by the Spanish renewable energy regulator REE (website accessed June 2018) shows that the Spanish parabolic trough fleet ran at about 26.5% capacity factor in 2017. This is not bad, especially as it is up from 21.8% in 2013 and has been rising steadily year-on-year, but most were originally expected to run above 30%. This may be partly due to reduced economic incentives as a result of retroactive changes to Spanish subsidies, which do not reward performance as much as originally intended. There are also legal limits to what operation and maintenance can be done on plants without invalidating the subsidy, and also changes to the rules on how much gas can be burned in the plant.

Indian pioneer Godawari Power & Ispat Ltd, which has a 50 MW parabolic trough plant in Gujarat commissioned in 2013, complained in its 2016 annual report that the site does not have the Direct Normal Insolation (direct sunshine) that it expected and therefore the Indian Central Electricity Regulatory Commission should pay it more for the power; it is not clear to me whose fault it is that the site is less sunny than expected, but Godawari did bid in 2010, in an auction where the average price for solar thermal was 11,480 rupees ($197)/MWh.

Figure 17.3, based on data collected by the Energy Information Administration for solar thermal plants in the US, shows the monthly output of US solar thermal plants compared with their predicted average monthly output (usually publically announced or released at the planning stage). Obviously, these plants should be generating more than their predicted average monthly output in the summer, and less in the winter.

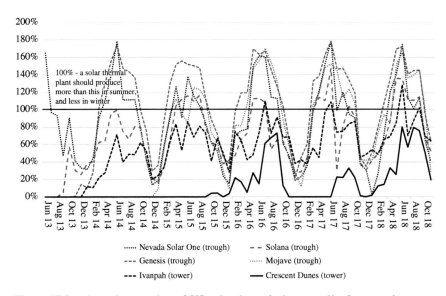

Figure 17.3.   Annual generation of US solar thermal plants, as % of expected average monthly generation.

*Source*: US Energy Information Administration, company releases before commissioning collected by the author (for expected production).

While the parabolic trough plants are generally producing electricity as predicted or close to it, it is noticeable that Ivanpah and Crescent Dunes — the two tower plants, built by Israel–US firm BrightSource and US-based SolarReserve, respectively — are not. Crescent Dunes in particular had a terrible 2017, offline entirely until July and then back to zero in December, though in late 2018 it did start to produce meaningful volumes (though not yet as much as originally planned). Ivanpah has generally done better, but still below specs, and uses a little more gas than originally anticipated, to get it started in the morning.

Spanish entrepreneur Belén Gallego, who has been involved with the sector for over a decade, remains a fan of solar thermal in general. "For sites with very clear skies and low seasonality [difference between winter and summer conditions], tower technologies are best, but conditions are make-or-break. You have to be looking at the specific site and the amount of aerosol in the air. And you need to focus mirrors from a kilometer away — if you are a hundredth of a degree off, you will miss the target. In the early days of the industry, this technology just didn't exist. In parabolic troughs the concentration happens a lot closer to where the heat transfer fluid is, so the air composition is not so critical."

This performance history does not deter solar thermal companies from bidding aggressively for new projects and promising significant price reductions. SolarReserve  signed a power purchase agreement for 78 Australian dollars ($61)/MWh in Australia to build the 150 MW Aurora Solar project, compared with $135/MWh it receives for the Crescent Dunes plant (which also received a federal loan and the US Investment Tax Credit). The precise economics of the Aurora project were not understood, and the project failed to secure financing and was cancelled in early 2019. SolarReserve also bid $64/MWh in July 2017 to supply 24-h power from a solar thermal project in the sunniest place on Earth, the Atacama Desert in Chile. However, SolarReserve has not yet, as of August 2018, won a power purchase agreement in Chile, being underbid by PV in the low $20s/MWh.

It may seem that I am lingering unfairly on the failures of a nascent industry. However, there are still major technical problems to be solved, and some of the cost figures that are being discussed by the solar industry do not seem to take this into account. No doubt the problems are solvable with enough investment — I am sure human ingenuity is capable of running a turbine on a distributed resource — but I would bet on a combination of PV and batteries, both of which actually work pretty reliably, to deliver much the same thing at lower cost in most places. So far, BloombergNEF's analysis supports this perspective.

One further intriguing possibility is to combine solar thermal with photovoltaics, using a small solar thermal field to charge a tank of molten salt in the daytime while the PV generates, and then turning on the turbine in the evening. The problem with this is potentially that the expensive turbine runs at a low capacity factor, but it may be possible to store multiple days' worth of heat in the salt for emergencies.

There are a few non-electrical uses of heat collected using solar thermal collectors. California-headquartered GlassPoint, for example, is building a huge field of parabolic collectors enclosed in a protective greenhouse, which will supply steam to an oilfield owned by Oman Petroleum. This will replace gas-heated steam used to extract more oil from difficult wells ('enhanced oil recovery'). The greenhouses are, according to the company, easy to clean and ensure that the parabolic troughs can be quite flimsy by design (since they do not have to stand up to wind load, or be cleaned). If the Oman plant works as expected, there will be other applications for solar heat for enhanced oil recovery. However, very often heat is a waste product in hot countries, and fossil fuel plants need significant amounts of water to cool them.

# Chapter 18

# Technology Focus: Photovoltaics

Crystalline silicon is the workhorse of the photovoltaic power industry, making up about 95% of the modules sold in 2017. There are only two significant companies supplying anything else, as of December 2018: US-headquartered First Solar Inc making cadmium telluride modules, and Japanese Solar Frontier KK making copper indium gallium selenide (CIGS) modules. Both are considered 'thin film' technologies, i.e. the process of making the modules involves depositing the semiconductor onto glass as a vapour and letting it crystallise in place in a layer a few microns thick. This is in contrast to the standard crystalline silicon type, where the semiconductor (silicon) is first crystallised into a block (ingot) and then cut it into slices at least 100 microns thick, a batch process with significant wastage (Table 18.1).

As of mid-2018, most of the smart money is on crystalline silicon. Professor Martin Green of the University of New South Wales, Director of the Australian Centre for Advanced Photovoltaics and sometimes called the 'father of modern photovoltaics', has conducted research on solar cell and module technologies since 1974. "People don't realise how stable silicon is" he says. "Some manufacturers are offering 30-year warranties on silicon products, and we expect this to go out to 50 years in the fullness of time". He is most optimistic about his group's search for the right material to be used in a tandem junction cell with silicon, increasing the cell efficiency by capturing more wavelengths of light (about half the efficiency of the layer underneath, plus the efficiency of the upper layer).

Table 18.1.  Types of solar module.

| Semiconductor | Crystalline silicon (c-Si) | Cadmium telluride (CdTe) thin film | Copper indium gallium selenide (CIGS or CIS) thin film | Amorphous silicon (a-Si) thin film | Organic, dye-sensitised, perovskite thin film |
|---|---|---|---|---|---|
| Approximate market share 2017 | 95% | 3% | 2% | 0% | 0% |
| Companies (2018) | Jinko, Trina, Suntech, etc | First Solar | Solar Frontier, Hanergy | Sharp, Powerfilm, Panasonic | Oxford PV |
| Status | Dominant | Competitive | Still in existence | Niche | In the lab |
| Advantages | Mature and cheap. No intrinsic degradation mechanism. Silicon is common and non-toxic. | No intrinsic degradation mechanism. Mature, bankable. Performs better (in kWh/kW/year terms) in low light and at high temperatures than c-Si. Probably cost competitive. Avoids import tariffs, which often refer specifically to c-Si. | No intrinsic degradation mechanism. Solar Frontier products are mature. Performs better (in kWh/kW/year terms) in low light than c-Si. Flexible products exist. Avoids import tariffs, which often refer specifically to c-Si. | Theoretically should be cheap. Good diffuse light performance. Excellent for calculator panels. Can be used in a tandem junction with c-Si for high efficiency (Panasonic's HIT modules. Flexible products exist. | Theoretically cheap. Some could be made into tandem modules with c-Si. |
| Disadvantages | Batch manufacturing process with some ungainly stages, like wafer slicing. Heavy and cannot be made flexible. | Only one company, so all cost reductions need to be done by that company. Double glass design is heavy. | Probably more expensive to manufacture than crystalline silicon. Single serious company is not growing. Lower efficiency (14–15%) than c-Si at present. | Few companies left. Intrinsic degradation mechanism. Many modules installed have been replaced a few years later with c-Si. Unlikely to be cost competitive. | Manufacturing at scale does not exist, nor (most likely) does the tech to deliver it exist as of 2018. Most have intrinsic degradation mechanisms. |

There is also no reason to stop at two layers. "20 or 30 years down the track, the next logical step is stacking more and more thin films onto a multi junction cell, increasing the efficiency more and more" he says.

## 18.1. Crystalline Silicon (c-Si) Photovoltaics

C-Si photovoltaics is based on silicon wafers. After the polysilicon has been made by the processes described in Chapter 6, it arrives at a further factory as a sack of chunks. It is then shaped into either multicrystalline or monocrystalline ingots, by melting it and allowing it to cool slowly, forming solids.

To grow a monocrystalline ingot, the crystal needs to grow very slowly into a single perfect block. A multicrystalline silicon ingot is made much faster, by allowing interlocking crystals to form from multiple nodes. As a rule, mono is a more efficient solar product, and has historically been more expensive.

The ingots are then sliced into wafers and 'doped' with phosphorus and boron, which change their electrical properties by making either free electrons or electron holes which respond when excited by light. The doped wafers are electrically connected and sealed into cells, then strung into modules. It is a batch process, i.e. one with relatively many complex steps in different types of factory, and over the years critics have claimed that this will be its downfall. So far, they are wrong.

C-Si technology has been around since 1954, when the first silicon-based solar cell, by Bell Labs, had an efficiency of 4%. While the fundamental technology today is the same, many individual tweaks make up the experience curve described in Chapter 7. The first wafers, for example, were small silicon discs a few centimetres across, while today's typical wafer is 150mm in diameter (and usually referred to as a six-inch wafer, although it's actually slightly smaller) and square. The silver paste used to make electrical connections has been improved and shaped more precisely, so that the busbars take up less of the active area of the cell without reducing electrical conductivity.

From 2016 to 2018, the process of making monocrystalline silicon wafers has been disrupted by diamond wire saws, which replace old-fashioned (or 'traditional' as one of my colleagues refers to them, which conjures up a delightful but misleading image of a cottage industry) wire saws using abrasive slurry containing silicon carbide. One of the major costs of wafer slicing with slurry is that roughly half the material is made into silicon sawdust ('kerf') and lost in the slurry, while the resulting wafers are thicker than they need to be to do their photoelectric job. Diamond wire saws are sharper, harder and can slice thinner while losing less in silicon sawdust, compared with slurry-based wire saws. As of December 2018, diamond wire saws have almost completely killed off slurry-based slicing, after coming to prominence just a few years earlier.

Other crystalline silicon innovations include tweaks to cell architecture to reduce electron–hole recombination, reduce reflection, or improve conductivity of current away from the cell. Bifacial modules will be discussed in Section 18.3.

## 18.2.  First Solar and the Thin Film Investment Bubble

First Solar and Solar Frontier's combined market share of about 5% of the global solar module market in 2018 represents almost all of the total success of a bubble in investor optimism for thin film technologies. Between 2006 and 2008, thin film solar companies raised over $2.5 billion in expansion capital, and for a while it seemed as if every Silicon Valley venture capitalist had to have one in their portfolio.

This enthusiasm for thin film was partly inspired by the success of First Solar itself at IPO in 2006, where the company raised $459 million after originally targeting $250 million, and saw its stock price soar. First Solar, however, was founded in 1990 and benefitted from over a decade of patience from investors including the Walton family (the owners of Wal-Mart). It was ready to hit mass production of an incredible 21.4 MW in 2005 (2017: 2,284 MW) when the German boom started and the silicon shortage began to bite crystalline silicon module makers.

First Solar has also shown incredible ability to meet its milestones and targets over the last 13 years, and has consistently communicated transparently and honestly. I'm almost sorry that in 2007, at an event held by trade promotion body Invest in Germany where the CEO of First Solar was speaking about the advantages of having a factory in Germany, I stood up and asked why their next planned factory was in Malaysia.

The CEO, Michael J Ahearn, was nice about it but I didn't get invited to the German embassy for drinks afterwards with the other participants.

As of late 2018, despite intense competition from crystalline silicon, First Solar has survived and is even thriving. In 2017 it reduced production to 2,284 MW from 3,097 MW in 2016, cutting output of its 'Series 4' module in order to accelerate production on its 'Series 6' module, which will be larger and hence easier to install. It has increased efficiency to that of an average multicrystalline silicon product (Figure 18.1).

For years, investment firms that had short seller positions on First Solar stock (and hence were hoping the stock price would plummet) published articles about the dangers of toxic cadmium and tellurium, imminent supply shortages, and other reasons to be fearful about the company. Very few of these stuck; there is no evidence that First Solar's modules are particularly likely to release toxic materials into the environment (cadmium telluride as a compound is in any case not as toxic as either of the elements which make it), the modules have consistently performed to specifications, and the company has effectively managed a module recycling programme, a large project development pipeline and a smooth scale-up.

It is unclear if cadmium telluride technology can continue to race crystalline silicon forever, but First Solar is making an excellent run of it.

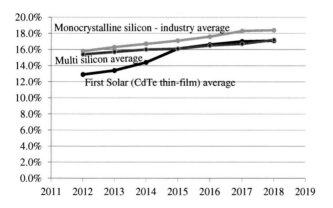

Figure 18.1.　Efficiencies of major solar module types.

*Note*: First Solar figures are for the fourth quarter of each year, except for 2018 when Q2 was the last reported at the time of writing.

*Source*: First Solar, BloombergNEF annual survey of module manufacturers.

It is winning contracts to supply large projects in the Middle East and Latin America at presumably competitive prices, while posting a profit in most quarters. As of late 2018 the company has also benefitted substantially from the trade war between China and the US heating up, meaning that there are import tariffs on all solar modules into the US. This makes First Solar modules an obvious choice for US projects.

It seemed perfectly logical in 2008 to back thin film technology, especially with First Solar making good profits and steadily increasing production. Silicon was expensive, and even if it became cheap, it did seem faintly ridiculous to continue with the crystalline silicon multi-step batch process involving sawing up blocks of semiconductor instead of laying it down directly. Most thin film technologies were less efficient than crystalline silicon, but as long as they promised lower costs per W, that didn't necessarily matter.

However, most of the other thin film companies were not, like First Solar, ready to begin mass production in 2005–2008. Astoundingly, it turned out to be more difficult than founders promised, and investors hoped, to control complex and very sensitive manufacturing processes. United Solar Ovonics (Unisolar), Konarka, Abound Solar, Odersun, Flexcell, Solyndra, Tokyo Electron and many others raised significant quantities of money for thin film between 2006 and 2013, but had exited the industry by 2014.

One problem is that it is vital to deposit the semiconductor in a uniform layer with consistent properties. If the active layer is patchy and uneven, the module will have the efficiency of the worst patch. Laying down semiconductor very evenly turns out to be quite difficult. Lab records for solar cells tend to be based on tiny scraps of active material, the best performing samples of a large bunch, and so a record set in the lab often does not translate to successful scale-up.

The other problem is almost unrelated to the choice of semiconductor, although those which require only low-temperature processes may be helpful. Many thin film companies have claimed that they will succeed through selling lightweight, flexible panels to niche applications such as weak roofs. Flexible panels could be manufactured continuously 'roll to roll', in theory, bringing down cost.

However, there is a reason why ordinary solar modules use glass as their major structural and moisture-resistant material — glass is excellent for this purpose. It's heavy, but it can last hundreds of years without losing its core properties of transparency and water resistance. Alternative encapsulants and front sheets are usually much worse at doing this, resulting in a product that degrades and underperforms — regardless of the semiconductor used. Since 70–80% of a solar panel's weight is glass (more for 'dual glass' designs which sandwich the active layers between two sheets of glass rather than using an opaque plastic backsheet), the semiconductor used makes very little difference to the weight.

There is a recognisable phase in the lifetime of an exotic semiconductor solar company that is not doing well. This is the phase where they say "our product is expensive and unlikely to last 25 years, but it is lightweight and flexible and will find niche markets in solar backpacks and aesthetically pleasing buildings" (or words to that effect). So far, these markets have yet to materialise. Even offgrid markets, where you might think a flexible lightweight product would make sense, prefer to use small amounts of inflexible but cheap and long-lived crystalline silicon. The only firm to achieve longevity in this niche is Iowa-based Powerfilm, which makes small volumes of flexible thin film silicon modules under contract to the US military. Most companies developing organic and dye-sensitised solar modules have reached this stage, and it usually immediately precedes either failure or stagnation.

Amorphous silicon also deserves a note of its own, although it is now seldom used for commercial modules. Amorphous silicon is made directly from silane gas, without going through the intermediate stage of polysilicon; it was hence unaffected by the shortage of purified polysilicon, as well as using a much thinner layer. It is the product used to power calculators since the 1970s, and is actually quite good for this, as it performs well in low light conditions such as indoors. Between 2006 and 2011, over 30 companies tried to make full-sized thin film silicon modules, 11 of them using manufacturing technology from Swiss material firm Oerlikon Solar and nine from US competitor Applied Materials [Chase, 2010]. Generally, these turnkey manufacturing plants were more difficult than anticipated to bring into production. Where they did sell modules, we have sometimes found evidence later that these were replaced with crystalline silicon (for example in Adani's 40 MW project in Kutch, India) — presumably due to very significant performance problems. Applied Materials discontinued sales of its Sunfab solar factory in June 2010, and Oerlikon Solar was first sold to Japanese Tokyo Electric in 2012 and then discontinued in 2014.

As of late 2018, the only commercial amorphous silicon product still on the market is Panasonic's 'Heterojunction with Intrinsic Thin layer' (HIT), a crystalline silicon product with an amorphous silicon layer. The two layers absorb different wavelengths of light, giving an overall higher efficiency than either alone (19.7%). It's a compelling proposal on paper, but technically nontrivial. Panasonic seems to have managed this, but its modules are expensive relative to plain crystalline silicon, and it does not appear to be planning a major scale up.

## 18.3. The Possible Module Technologies of the Future

The most-hyped potential breakthrough technology of late 2018 is perovskites. These are semiconductors based on lead compounds. The reason researchers are excited is that, between 2011 and 2016, they went from being unknown to 22% efficient in the lab, an incredibly rapid progression of technical performance. They also have light absorption properties that would make them a good fit for tandem junction with crystalline silicon.

However, perovskites still have short lifetimes and have not been manufactured in bulk, as of late 2018. Martin Green was initially optimistic about them as the second layer in a tandem cell with silicon, but as of mid-2018 he says, "I was hoping to get rid of the lead, but it's been hopeless; in anything without lead, the efficiency drops well below 10%. Progress with perovskite stability has been incremental but not exponential." He is currently more excited about copper zinc tin sulfate semiconductors as a potential second layer.

It is possible that someone flicking through this book in 2030 will marvel at my failure to anticipate their perovskite-powered world, but it's equally possible that the solar industry will achieve vast scale just with crystalline silicon. Also, as an analyst, you can achieve a remarkably high success rate with predictions just by being skeptical of the next big thing, especially when it looks a lot like things that have already failed.

Organic and dye-sensitised PV are other options, using semiconductors which are polymers or carbon-based compounds. They have been around for at least a decade in the lab, without making obvious progress towards commercialisation. Most at present have much too short a lifetime to use in a commercial product.

Crystalline silicon is far from done reducing solar module costs. Perovskites, organic and dye-sensitised PV or another breakthrough technology *could* come and eat the lunch of crystalline silicon manufacturing companies. But the c-Si manufacturers are competing fiercely with one another to make better products for lower prices, and breakthrough technologies will have to beat their best efforts to be worth using.

Perhaps the most interesting new module type to market participants in 2018 is bifacial solar modules. These are, quite simply, modules (usually crystalline silicon) where instead of an opaque plastic backsheet, a second sheet of glass is used, so that they are transparent from behind. This means they can capture reflected light as well as direct light, giving at least a 10% bonus in some situations (such as when the modules are mounted over a reflective surface like sand or water). Apparently the improvement is up to 90% on snow, although there cannot be many places where a module will receive long hours of sunlight against a snowy backdrop.

## 18.4. Innovations in How the Modules Are Installed

There are several ways to optimise how photovoltaic systems are designed, whatever module you use.

The simplest is to change the ratio between the size of the inverter (the alternating current or AC rating of the system) and the size of the modules (the DC rating). This essentially caps the maximum power output from the modules. Figure 18.2 shows what this might do to the output of a photovoltaic system on a sunny day in Germany.

Why might one make a design decision that limits the maximum output of the system? Part of the reason is that you get slightly more output when the sun is not at its maximum (the 'shoulder periods'), because inverters are more efficient close to their maximum capacity. If the capacity of solar modules is fixed, a smaller inverter will activate

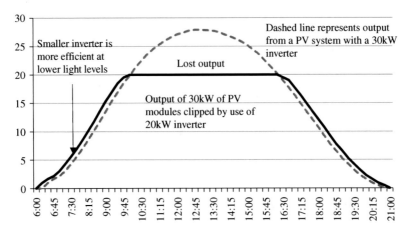

Figure 18.2.   Illustrative power output, in kW, from 30 kW of modules on a sunny day. If the inverter is also 30 kW, there will be no clipping (but maximum power output probably never hits the full 30 kW). If the inverter is only 20 kW, there will be some loss of generated energy.

(i.e. the system will start generating) slightly earlier in the morning as the sun rises than a larger inverter would, and switch off slightly later at night. However, the main reason is simply that there are not many really sunny days in Germany, so the power lost may not be worth paying extra for a larger inverter. (As of BloombergNEF's PV Market Outlook in the third quarter of 2018, we estimate that an inverter costs about 4 US cents of the typical 89 cent cost per W (DC) of a utility scale system. We assumed that this typical system had a module capacity of 1.25 of its inverter capacity, i.e. an inverter loading ratio of 1.25 [Bromley *et al.*, 2018]).

Modules can also be installed on 'tracking systems', motorised mounting structures which follow the sun across the sky. While these can rotate on two axes to follow the sun both high and low, most trackers are single axis, i.e. they just turn from east to west facing every day. This increases the output from the modules by roughly 20–30% compared to a stationary system. A second axis increases this slightly more, but also adds the complication of a second set of motors, which doubles the chance of a failure. Tracking systems increase operation and maintenance costs slightly because moving parts fail more easily than fixed ones, but the increase is worth it in sunny places where the 20–30% increase in generation is substantial.

Tracking systems increase generation in the morning and the evening, giving a wider shoulder to the generation shown in Figure 18.2. This can be particularly valuable in places where there is already a lot of fixed solar, and power at midday is no longer of peak value. Tracking extends the period of high generation later into the afternoon, meeting demand for power for air conditioning for longer. Most large-scale PV systems being built in the US as of 2018 use tracking, partly for this reason. By contrast, hardly any of the PV systems in China use tracking, mainly because they are compensated at the same rate regardless of time of generation. Northern Europe is not sunny enough to warrant tracking systems, although many recently built German rooftop systems are oriented slightly west, to increase generation in the evening when the owners will be home to use the electricity directly.

Designing a PV system to increase air flow across the module can reduce the typical operating temperature of the module, and increase output. The main reason for this is that crystalline silicon solar modules lose between 0.2% and 0.6% of their efficiency for every degree Celsius above the 25°C standard operating temperature. High temperatures can also increase degradation.

## 18.5. Toxicity

Solar, wind and battery technologies are not completely free from environmental impacts. Wind farms do kill some birds, and magnets in the nacelle (hub bit in the middle of a wind turbine) use the rare material neodymium, mostly mined in China. The most popular types of battery contain lithium and cobalt, which must be mined; 60% of cobalt production is in the Democratic Republic of the Congo [Frith *et al.*, 2018], where there are legitimate concerns about conditions and use of child labour in mines.

Dustin Mulvaney, Associate Professor at the Environmental Studies Department at San José State University, first became interested in the question of solar's environmental impacts during his postdoctoral training. "In Silicon Valley at the time, there were 12–15 thin-film manufacturers, mostly copper indium gallium selenide but some cadmium telluride. The semiconductor industry has left a pretty bad legacy of pollution in

California, and my interest was in the consequences of this next generation of technology companies coming to the Valley." His research, in 2011, found cadmium compounds in wastewater exported out of the state as hazardous waste by solar companies that were not yet in commercial production. However, he says, "within a year, all those companies were gone" — in some cases due to market conditions, in others because of low manufacturing yields. Crystalline silicon solar panels do not contain cadmium at all, and CdTe survivor First Solar has proper measures in place at its factories, and provisions to recycle its panels at the end of their lives.

Mulvaney continues to study environmental health and safety issues around the life cycle of clean energy technologies. "All the issues around toxic materials used in solar are completely manageable" he says.

There are two times in a solar panel's life where management of materials is critical: at the beginning and at the end. In the middle — at least 25 years and probably longer in most cases — solar panels sit in the sun being inert and encapsulated.

Crystalline silicon modules are not especially toxic; the vast bulk of them is glass, aluminium, plastic, and silicon wafer. The most dangerous component is the lead in the solder used to make electrical connections in most modules, although SunPower has found a way to avoid using this. To put it into perspective, a German study by the Stuttgart Institute of Photovoltaics [Feifel *et al.*, 2018] estimated that the total lead contained in solar panels installed up to the end of 2016 was 11,000 tonnes. The International Lead Association estimates that as of 2012, annual lead use for ammunition is 150,000 tonnes/year. I do not know how much of the lead in ammunition is recycled.

Solar panel recycling is in its infancy, but the main reason for this is that over 99.7% of solar panels ever installed are still in use. European industry group PVCycle, founded in 2007, offers a take-back and recycling service which recycles 90–97% of the material in used panels. In Europe, producers are responsible for funding collection and recycling under amendments made to the Waste Electrical and Electronic Equipment Directive in 2012. PVCycle has recycled just under 20,000 tonnes of panels as of 2017, and 4,153 tonnes in that year. It opened a new treatment site for used and discarded solar panels near Aix-en-Provence, France, in 2018.

Solar manufacturing involves more hazardous materials, and can pose a risk to worker health and safety. There are two examples which form the basis of any news article desperately working a 'solar is actually bad' angle. One occurred in March 2008, when the polysilicon boom was at its height and spot prices were over $400/kg. A Washington Post article detailed how a Chinese company called Luoyang Zhonggui was dumping corrosive silicon tetrachloride on fields near local villages, causing respiratory problems to the inhabitants. The pollution was a result of the inexperienced company's poor implementation of closed-loop silicon tetrachloride recycling. Established silicon manufacturers process the silicon tetrachloride back into hydrochloric acid and silane feedstock, reducing the need to buy more of these expensive inputs. The Chinese government took measures in 2011 to close down companies without 98.5% silicon tetrachloride recycling. Even before that, the fall in the price of polysilicon after 2008 made manufacture without closed-loop recycling wildly uneconomic. They can't still be dumping silicon tetrachloride, because it's valuable, and there has been no further news of that type of pollution incident after 2008.

The other example is the mess left by Abound Solar, a US manufacturer of CdTe modules which went bankrupt in July 2012. According to local newspaper the Denver Post, costs for cleaning up the cadmium-contaminated factory, encasing leftover cadmium materials in concrete and sending leftover panels to First Solar for recycling were estimated at between $2.2 and $3.7 million. Presumably, these were paid and the factory cleaned up, since it was bought by electric cooperative United Power in 2018.

Of course the industry must act responsibly in producing and managing the materials needed to make solar panels and other components of clean energy; but it is, in general, already doing so. Best practice in manufacturing processes, worker safety and recycling will continue to evolve with the industry.

# Chapter 19

# Operating Solar Plants, and How Big Data Can Help

Chapter 14 on the cost of energy assumed that the running cost of a PV plant is negligible, which is good enough for a first approximation. The beauty of PV is that it sits in the sun and generates energy with very little interference, and most plants (with the exception of those using tracking) have no moving parts to break.

For completeness, however, it is worth discussing operational costs. Of course things can go wrong with a PV plant, and if you want it to continue generating electricity, these need to be fixed. Homeowners in particular often pay little attention to whether their solar panels are performing as promised once they are up, and this is a pity from an energy production perspective and for their finances. Some firms already do track performance and send the homeowner an update, but so far most seem to charge quite a lot for it.

Solar panels do get dirty, and in extreme cases can lose nearly all their output. My parents' home system in the damp UK accumulates a thick growth of algae, and a birch tree which has grown up since they installed it in 2010 is blocking their sunlight during the most productive hours. In Germany, many solar plants are not cleaned at all, instead relying on rainfall to wash off dust and dry weather to scorch off the algae. Ground-mounted solar plants in places where it rains need 'vegetation management', i.e. mowing the grass and cutting down the trees and bushes before they start to shade the panels. Usually this is done with machinery, but sheep, goats and geese can also do the job provided the plant has been designed so that they cannot access any cables. (Geese and goats will chew right through fairly heavy electrical cables just for fun.) In very arid climates, vegetation is less of a concern, but dust is more so; some US solar projects use special dust-settling sprays around their sites. In the Middle East, the dust is a particular problem as very fine stuff blows in off the Sahara desert and is hard to remove, caking up when water is used.

This is another potential issue: solar plants do use water, though less than energy generation technologies which use heat to produce steam or for cooling. The International Energy Agency estimated in a 2012 report entitled *Water for Energy: Is energy becoming a thirstier resource?* that most gas, coal and nuclear plants use about 1,000–10,000 L of water per MWh generated, compared with about 100 L/MWh for a photovoltaic plant. All these figures can be reduced; gas plants can also be dry cooled (resulting in lower efficiency of converting fuel into electricity) to use around 10 L/MWh, and PV panels can also be dry cleaned with a brush, using almost no water. It's safe to say that washing PV uses an order of magnitude less water per MWh than most other generation technologies, although naturally solar plants in desert countries tend to be located in water-poor areas that are not valuable for agriculture.

Historically, solar plant operators have gone low tech when it comes to cleaning. In the Middle East, the preferred technology is a bunch of people with brushes, going around at night scrubbing the panels. A few plants using tracking technology are designed so the panels align themselves correctly and then a truck drives up and down the rows rinsing and rubbing, like a carwash in reverse. In future, panel cleaning robots like those made by Israeli firm Ecoppia may do this labour-intensive, low-skilled and not particularly satisfying work. Perhaps the union battles of 2030 will be between striking solar cleaners and the robots.

The other major component of operation and maintenance of solar plants is fixing or replacing the electronics when they go wrong. The most point of failure is the inverter, although cables, modules and junction boxes can corrode. In the past it was usual to replace the whole inverter, even for very large inverters which require a big truck to take them on and off the site, but now there are more likely to be exchangeable components which can be swapped out once a problem is diagnosed.

If a few modules fail, it is best to replace them as exactly as possible with the same. This gets more difficult as the power rating (efficiency) of new modules drifts up, and sometimes you may need to move all the good old modules onto the same string. The new warranty replacement modules then need to be installed on a different string. This is a lot of work, and it is really desirable that the modules not fail.

The effect of these costs on plant economics becomes increasingly obvious as solar power gets cheaper (i.e. the capex falls). A normal full-service operation and maintenance (O&M) contract between a solar plant owner and an O&M service company in 2018 costs about $10,000–20,000/MW/year, covering monitoring, cleaning, security, vegetation management, preventative maintenance and replacement of broken parts [Hayim, 2018]. If the plant has a capacity factor of 20%, this is $6–12/MWh just in O&M, which seemed irrelevant when solar power cost hundreds of dollars per MWh but becomes critical when prices are below $50/MWh. Indeed, as of early 2018 I remain skeptical of solar power prices below $30 for this reason; I think developers are making optimistic assumptions about how well a solar plant in a dusty environment will perform with minimal maintenance, and they may be planning to sell the project before some of the challenges become fully apparent.

These operational costs are unlikely to see enormous improvements in the next 10 years. There are, however, ways in which technology can help at least a little. It is now quite common to identify the solar modules which have electrical manufacturing defects called 'hotspots' by flying a drone with an infrared camera over the field. Analyzing the images to spot modules with minor problems allows them to be replaced at the convenience of the contractor and the bill sent to the module manufacturer's warranty department. The equipment to monitor the solar plants is also becoming increasingly sophisticated, collecting data at short intervals for every string of modules, which is fed back to a central processing hub. This data can be used to reduce unnecessary maintenance work, for example by telling the contractor company exactly when cleaning the panels will be cost-effective to optimise generation or revenue for the cost, or indicating which components may be in pre-failure modes so spares can be ordered and repair staff can schedule site visits on a non-emergency basis.

The other major reason why O&M costs for solar plants have come down (and, anecdotally, the prices were higher than $50,000/MW/year in 2008, compared with under $20,000/MW/year a decade later) is that as the prices paid for solar power comes down, it is not worth paying a huge premium to get a contractor who will instantly respond to problems. If 2% of your solar plant is not operational because a chip fried in the inverter, it's unlikely to kill anyone (unlike in some other types of generation plant) and it will not black out half a city. This means there is no longer a strong incentive to keep duplicate components on site and engineering staff on call. If the problem can be fixed in a few days, that's probably good enough. In general, PV plants are not rocket science or nuclear engineering. They are meant to sit in the sun generating electricity without interference, and generally well-designed plants do.

Other major running costs of a large solar plant include insurance — around 0.5% of capex per year — security against theft, and management fees. Security measures range from a large fence to a constant patrol of dogs, to prevent theft. Thieves used to take the modules for re-sale, but now modules are less valuable, they are more likely to go for the copper cables which have a much better value to weight ratio. Between 2013 and 2018 the choice of material for the bulk of PV plant cables switched from copper to aluminium, simply because copper prices rose on the world market and became a target. Replacing stolen cables is both expensive and extremely tedious.

Management fees pay for services like billing the power buyer, making sure O&M contractors get paid, and re-negotiating contracts. They probably have significant room to be brought down by software and by aggregating portfolios to have them run by one company. A PV management company might never actually visit the site, but have effective ways to track performance and problems remotely.

Occasionally something does go seriously wrong at a solar plant, for example a tornado smashing through the site, or failure of a large number of modules. The latter would usually be covered by accident insurance. Module failure should be covered by the supplier warranty, but often the supplier has gone out of business and the investor may lose money replacing them. This appears to have happened with a number of thin film silicon modules installed between 2005 and 2015.

A last talking point, as of 2018, is that solar plants can have more than the minimum amount of biodiversity. Since they are not substantially disturbed for over 25 years, they can be managed as a low-lying, shaded wildflower meadow, providing habitat and food for pollinating insects. This can improve productivity of crops on the surrounding farms, and increase the general resilience of the local ecosystem.

# Chapter 20

# Trade Wars

Over the last 50 years, Asian economies have become better and better at producing all sorts of goods — plastic trinkets, shoes and clothes, semiconductor chips and computer hardware — for a low cost. The exact dynamics change over time — I remember in the late 1980s, 'Made in Japan' was considered low quality at least in my corner of rural England, while now 'Made in Japan' is a stamp of pride from a high-tech economy considered one of the most developed in the world. Perhaps in 2050 we will look at Vietnam or Indonesia as similar pinnacles of technological achievement.

In general, Europe and the US have enjoyed the rising availability of cheap semiconductor chips, computers, headphones and other electronics from Taiwan, China and increasingly Malaysia and the Philippines. Aside from occasional concern for the conditions of workers, there has been very little backlash; going back to making everything in America or Europe now would be disruptive and politically unpalatable to consumers who are used to being able to buy cheap. The story from the economist's perspective is that well-educated workers in the US and Europe will have to continue to innovate to stay ahead, while by the time the workers in Asia have caught up on skills, they will be demanding similar salaries and working conditions.

Occasionally though, an industry does fight back — and there is legislation allowing it to do this. The argument is that if a nation secures a leading position in the manufacture of a good then it can drive competitors out of business, destroy industries in competing countries, and then once it no longer has competition, put its prices up.

The allegation behind a trade war is that a government has deliberately subsidised industries to offer prices that make no profit, and are intended to drive foreign competition out of business and secure a monopoly position (presumably, to then raise prices again). This is called 'subsidisation', and leads to 'dumping', which is selling products at a loss or at a price lower than in their home market (both definitions of dumping are valid). Examples of goods on which the European Commission has opened investigations include 'certain concrete reinforcement bars and rods', 'Polyester yarn (high tenacity)', 'Hand pallet trucks', 'Footwear with uppers of leather (certain)' from Vietnam, and 'Ring binder mechanisms (certain)' from Thailand. There are lawyers in Brussels with large files about too-cheap ring binders.

In practice, it is seldom obvious what subsidies are unfair, and the cases keep many lawyers in good wine and expensive dinners. China's government does offer incentives to manufacturers to set up factories in industries the government considers strategic — for example, free land in a new industrial estate, tax breaks, cheap power from state-owned utilities, or lines of credit from state-owned banks. But so does the government in nearly every country, certainly in the US and Europe. When an international company wishes to set up a factory — creating jobs — it can usually shop around for the best offer on where to put the factory, and country and local governments have people on payroll to conduct these negotiations on their behalf. The governments can then boast about the creation of 'green jobs'.

When it is an American offer, it is considered by Americans to be vital strategic support to accelerate development of the industry of the future and create jobs. When it is a Chinese offer, Americans consider this to be illegal subsidisation with the aim of dumping product and destroying American jobs. The European Commission is somewhat more evenhanded, although it also runs interminable investigations. The World Trade Organization (WTO) acts as a sort of international arbiter.

The redress within a country is managed by the Department of Commerce or equivalent, and often takes the form of a tax ('anti-dumping' and 'anti-subsidy' tariffs) on imports from the country accused of dumping or subsidisation. Individual companies — for example, Chinese manufacturers of solar modules — are invited to submit information about the government subsidies they have received, from which individual anti-dumping and anti-subsidy rates are calculated by the company. Manufacturers which do not cooperate by submitting information get a single, much higher tariff rate.

There is often negotiation, with the importing country using anti-dumping and anti-subsidy tariffs as a stick. For example, in Europe in 2013, Chinese manufacturers negotiated an 'Undertaking' with the European Commission whereby they would sell solar modules only at or above a 'Minimum Import Price', and in exchange would not pay the import tariffs, set at least 37.2%. This Minimum Import Price was adjusted based on changes to BloombergNEF's Spot Price Index, rather to my trepidation as it created an incentive for companies to submit biased data to our price survey, which we had to take measures to counter. (Mostly, we requested to see recent contracts from companies applying to join the survey, and from companies submitting unusually high or low results. We also relied heavily on getting quotes from both buyers and sellers of components, so that hopefully subtle biases would cancel out, and wildly exceptional values identified and removed.)

Sometimes negotiations fail and countries end up taking punitive measures. In 2011, the US agreed to set trade tariffs on imports of Chinese solar modules. China responded by setting trade tariffs on US polysilicon imports, which was devastating to US manufacturers Hemlock Semiconductor and REC Silicon. The whole affair was also inconvenient to Chinese buyers of US polysilicon and to US module buyers, all of which had to pay more.

The problem with using trade tariffs as a weapon is that there is usually a legal loophole. Chinese solar modules could initially be shipped to a third country such as Thailand, re-labelled as Product of Thailand, and re-exported to the US and the EU without penalty. Then lawyers for the local manufacturers bring an 'anti-circumvention' case to court, and often the loophole is closed. By 2018, Chinese module manufacturers had set up extensive factories in Vietnam, Thailand, India and other countries to beat trade tariffs, and also to avoid ever-increasing labour cost and turnover in China. (One manufacturer noted in 2016 that in Jiangsu, a lively Chinese solar manufacturing hub, they were losing about 10% of their factory workforce each month to competitors — meaning hiring and training replacements was a constant battle). Polysilicon manufacturers cannot relocate so easily, and so Hemlock and REC Silicon continue to suffer from the closure of the Chinese market to them. As far as I can tell, the main beneficiaries of the solar trade war have been trade lawyers, which is admittedly a form of 'green job'.

As of late 2018, the US government is doubling down on the trade war with China, and has implemented new tariffs adding about 9 cents/W to the price of a 23-cent/W module. It has had little obvious positive effect on manufacturers in the US; one of the firms which filed the trade case, Suniva, has gone bankrupt. US-headquartered First Solar has benefitted, but mainly because the trade case specifies crystalline silicon, and so First Solar's cadmium telluride modules are exempt wherever they were made. The companies which suffer are not so much the Chinese manufacturers — which are in any case busy supplying their domestic market — as the developers and installers in the US, who pay higher prices and pass them on to their customers.

The European Commission dropped its measures against Chinese modules in September 2018. India, however, is now also considering taxes on all imports. Trade wars are likely to be an annoying drag on the solar industry for years to come.

# Chapter 21

# Will Offgrid Solar Leapfrog in the Developing World?

We have not yet discussed the first, most intuitive, once and perhaps future largest market for solar panels. This is the world beyond the existing power grid, where solar competes with candles or kerosene for producing light, and with diesel generators for producing electricity.

One of the earliest groups of buyers for unsubsidised solar was in Norway, where many families own a cabin ('hytte') up in the wilds where they holiday in the summer. These cabins are remote even for deliveries of diesel, and presumably the hum of a diesel generator spoils the tranquility. The electricity needs of the cabin are small, just a few lights for the few dark hours of the Norwegian summer and maybe a small television, which can be handled with a modest solar panel and a battery. So, in the 1980s and 1990s, Norwegians bought some of the few MW of solar panels sold per year, and presumably still do, with the market limited only by the small number of cabins. Some allotments in Switzerland have the same system, a small solar panel to charge a battery so that summer barbecues can be lit into the night.

For many people, however, being off the electricity grid is not a charming back-to-nature leisure choice. As of early 2018, the Global Offgrid Lighting Association (GOGLA) estimated that 2.2 billion people worldwide have no access to reliable electricity. If they want light at night, their historical options are candles or kerosene lamps, which are expensive and also produce particulate matter and soot, which harms the human respiratory system.

One option is to extend the power grid to every house, as has been done in most developed countries. However, grid extension costs money, often a lot of money where people are widely dispersed, to serve people who currently have extremely low power usage. Often, people will walk tens of kilometres several times a week to charge a phone at a privately owned diesel generator. A much cheaper way to get those people basic electricity supply — enough for light at night, mobile phone charging, even a small television — can be to use solar and batteries in some combination. For example, a solar-powered lantern can be sold for under $5 in 2018, and give a household basic light and phone charging for hours after sunset.

The problem is always paying for it. Many people find the money to buy 20 cents' worth of kerosene every week, but might struggle to put together $5 for a solar lantern, even if it would pay back within a year. It is very difficult to save money when there is no banking system.

British fantasy author Terry Pratchett described this problem as the 'Boots' theory of socio-economic injustice: a rich man might buy a pair of boots costing $50, which last him 10 years (this is not the time to quibble about the exact lifespan of boots. Maybe I'm buying insufficiently expensive boots). A poor man might have to buy a cheap pair of boots costing $10, which last 1 year. After 5 years, he has spent as much as the rich man, and he still sometimes has wet feet.

To develop Pratchett's idea: one solution is to give the poor man some good boots. Or you could give him $50, and he might buy good boots, or something he felt he needed even more, like shoes for his children or mosquito nets. (There's also some evidence that if you're giving anyone in developing countries money, you should give it to the women of a community first as they are less likely to spend it on alcohol and cigarettes than the men, which is sexist but possibly true.) A further alternative, if you are not sufficiently philanthropic to hand over $50, or want to help more people with that $50, is to lend the man the money to buy good boots. At 10% interest rate, he still pays it off in 7 years with what he would have spent on bad boots and has 3 more years of dry feet, assuming nobody nicks his boots.

Microfinance is a key word in circles focused on reducing poverty in developing countries. It means lending small amounts of money — enough for a handcart or an irrigation pump or a solar lantern — at interest rates which can be up to 25%. This often does not fully compensate the lender for the risk (in our boots analogy, the risk is that someone nicks the good boots from the borrower, or the borrower takes the boots and runs far away). This is particularly true in the early stages of setting up a microfinance scheme when the cost to find the customer and set up the loan is very high. However, it can come down rapidly with scale. It may be difficult to find the first customer, explain the concept of a loan, do your best due diligence on them, and arrange a mechanism to collect payments, but once the idea spreads it will be easier to lend to the 100th person.

Mobile phones have spread rapidly across Africa, and made life much more convenient for people with very little. A report by the Pew Research Center in 2015 found that 65% of Ugandans owned a cellphone, 73% of Tanzanians, and 83% of Ghanaians (the percentage has doubtless risen since). These are used not just for chatting, but for small-scale commerce — to check the prices at the market before making the long trek to buy or sell, or to find out if a required item is available in a place without going there. And they are used for banking. Many countries in Africa have a network of kiosks, which will sell phone credit, and this can be used as a currency and transferred with a few clicks.

This enables more complex methods of financing solar lanterns and larger solar home systems. For example, you can sell a solar lantern on a payment plan, where the initial cost is low but an inbuilt chip makes the lantern ineffective if the user does not regularly transfer payments to the giver by mobile phone. This means that the user can make their usual kerosene payments (or often lower payments) to the solar lantern distributor instead, getting cleaner light, and after a year or two have paid off the solar lantern and hopefully have several more years of free light. It also means that if the lantern does get stolen, the borrower cannot be held liable for the debt (although there is usually a downpayment which they lose, and their embryonic credit rating will be affected). As of 2018, solar lanterns have got so cheap that microfinance providers are generally trying to fund larger solar systems for homes and small businesses.

Another option for poverty reduction using solar is a straight giveaway of solar lanterns. These are somewhat controversial. Occasionally organisations decide to do this, and in acute situations such as in refugee camps it is the easiest option to give people very basic energy access (i.e. light, phone charging). However, where the problem of poor energy access is chronic rather than acute, giveaways can do harm as well as good. For example, the supply of a large volume of solar lanterns is usually tendered out to the lowest bidder, and since it is very difficult to control quality in bulk purchases, there is a risk that the products do not last long and give the users a poor impression of the technology's potential to help them. It also suppresses the development of local distribution networks selling solar lanterns for profit. Canada-headquartered solar project developer SkyPower announced in 2015 that it would give away 2 million solar lanterns in Kenya and 1.5 million in Bangladesh, and was criticised by GOGLA for this decision.

Solar lanterns are also extremely basic energy access; few of us would be satisfied with a trickle of light for the evenings and the ability to charge a non-smart phone. However, they are only the start. Already, slightly larger solar panel and battery systems are available off-the-shelf, and can be linked together to provide more energy as a household's energy needs expand. A specialised market for reasonable-performance but low-energy-use TVs, fans and other devices (usually running off direct current rather than alternating current) is developing to serve these households. The better the efficiency of a device, the smaller the solar and battery system need to be to power it.

GOGLA estimates that its members sold about 3.7 million units of solar electrified lighting in the first half of 2018, with the number of products sold increasing slowly and the average size increasing fast. The average system cost was about $60, possibly not representative of the entire market as GOGLA members are often headquartered in Europe or the US, using branding and technology to make a differentiated product. These face competition from China-made generic products, which can provide the same service at a lower price. Cheaper products might break sooner — but then again, they might not.

If a whole village has power off the central electricity grid, it is currently likely to run on a diesel generator. These have low upfront cost (capex) but high running costs (opex), as the diesel needs to be transported to the village. Often the village can save money by adding a solar panel (or two or 20) and a battery to reduce the amount of diesel consumed. The battery is particularly useful, because diesel generators run very inefficiently when not at their maximum power output. With a battery, even if the solar panels fail to keep it charged, the diesel generator can run for a short time at high efficiency to recharge it. Sometimes the solar and battery system can be financed by investors expecting to make a return from selling power, particularly if there is an 'anchor customer' such as a shop or a mine, who contracts to buy a portion of the power production for an agreed price. This reduces the risk that the system will work perfectly but nobody pays for the power. A firm called Redavia ameliorates this risk by renting out PV systems which can be packed up and redeployed if necessary, although it would presumably prefer to leave them *in situ*. Redavia has projects in Ghana and Tanzania so far.

A major risk to financing microgrid systems is that the main electricity grid may be extended to the village, rendering the microgrid's output expensive and obsolete. This risk is dropping as the cost of solar and batteries falls closer to the price of power from the grid, and in some countries the grid suffers frequent outages. However, it is a small irony that the possibility of a village being connected to the grid in future may impair its ability to get a microgrid financed today. Governments can help by communicating grid extension plans well in advance.

I am very optimistic about the ability of solar and batteries to eventually provide a high level of energy service to people who currently lack it, leapfrogging the need for new grid and new power stations. Investors are also optimistic, investing $156 million in 2015, $223 million in 2016 and $265 million in 2017 in offgrid energy access companies. In 2016, BloombergNEF carved offgrid access away from solar information in its coverage into a separate topic called Frontier Power, tracking activity in providing power to people and places with no or limited access to electricity.

# Chapter 22

# Can Solar Save the World?

I'm going to assume that the reader already has serious concerns about climate change caused by humans burning fossil fuels. If not, it is unlikely that I can say much to convince you; it is the biggest challenge to humanity of this century, likely to have serious impacts in all kinds of unanticipated ways and kill millions of people. This chapter will focus on whether solar can make a meaningful contribution to the world's energy supply so we can continue to use power, and have the standard of living we have come to expect, without digging stuff up and burning it.

The conclusion of this chapter is that solar is unlikely to be able to eliminate energy sector carbon dioxide emissions by itself. However, it can help.

## 22.1. Direct Effects of Solar

Some rough calculations for a solar system being added to our current electricity grid: an ordinary 4 kW household PV system in the UK produces around 3,854 kWh/year (an 11% capacity factor). A typical household in the UK in 2016 used 3,900 kWh of electricity per year (plus the equivalent of 13,800 kWh of gas for cooking and heating), according to UK energy regulator Ofgem, so a PV system of this size would make the average household roughly a net zero electricity exporter/consumer over the year. On the other hand, total electricity generation in the country was 337.7 TWh in 2015 (according to UK Department of Energy and

Climate Change statistics), which divided by the population of 65.6 million (UK Office of National Statistics, 2016), means the average annual UK electricity generation including commercial, industrial and office use is about 5,150 kWh/person — much more than just their household use, since the average household contains more than one person.

How much carbon dioxide equivalent would the PV system save? Well, the average carbon intensity of UK electricity generation was, according to the UK government, 332g/kWh in 2015. So, if PV is replacing average kWh of electricity generation, this 4 kW system will save 1.2 tonnes of carbon emissions per year. (The carbon cost of producing the modules is a complex calculation, but is probably negligible; most academic estimates put the energy payback time of manufacturing a solar module at 1–3 years, and they are under warranty for 25 years and should last longer.)

Is 1.2 tonnes of savings a lot? Well, at least according to climatecare. org (an online carbon offset calculator — there are many, but they do give approximately the same results, with the proviso that it depends enormously on assumptions made on factors beyond your control, such as how many seats on a flight are empty), it's roughly the same as a return flight in economy class from London to New York, which is less impressive. A similar solar system in California would generate more energy — about 7,000 kWh/year — because it is sunnier, but the California generation system is less carbon-intensive, so this would save about 1.7 tonnes by this extremely crude methodology. Californians also use more electricity, on average, than people in the UK.

So, adding a few solar panels is not going to completely end the damage we are doing to our world. Can it at least take a good chunk out of our energy-related emissions, which are still substantial (Figure 22.1)?

Just 10 years ago, scepticism was warranted. David MacKay was mildly scathing about solar in his 2008 book *Sustainable Energy — Without the Hot Air* (mine is the 2016 revised edition) although he did conclude that solar power in deserts had the technical potential to supply the UK and other places with the 125 kWh/day he estimated we need altogether. He suggested that "countries that have enough land and sunshine to spare should host a big bake-off contest between solar chimneys and concentrating solar power, to be funded by oil-producing and

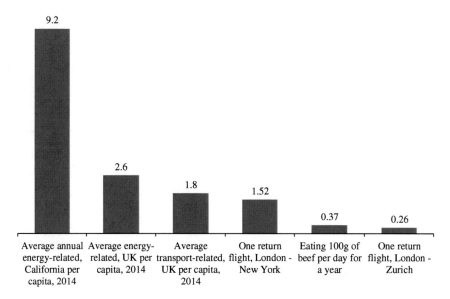

Figure 22.1.   Carbon dioxide emission equivalent of various human activities (metric tonnes).

*Sources*: US Energy Information Agency, climatecare.org, UK Government Statistical Release 2016, Beef Production and Greenhouse Gas Emissions by Avery & Avery, Environmental Health Perspective, September 2008.

oil-consuming countries", which is not a bad idea, except that these days PV seems a far more plausible technology to get energy from deserts (and solar chimneys are still not a thing). Politically, however, running a large wire from Europe down to North Africa, or even joining up the United States internally with a strong power grid, is still a very long way away.

David MacKay's book made a couple of valid points; we use a lot more energy (particularly when non-electrical consumption is included) than can easily be supplied by UK rooftop PV and wind. Nuclear is an obvious way to supply a useful chunk of energy without emitting much carbon dioxide or relying on scarce resources; indeed, since 2008, leading environmentalists such as George Monbiot have become pro-nuclear, largely because climate change is more terrifying than radiation (more on nuclear at the end of this chapter). Overall, David MacKay's book argued against the idea that we can consume all the resources we like if we simply build a few wind turbines and solar panels, and this is still an accurate argument.

A couple of things have happened since 2008, however, which leave room for optimism. Firstly, MacKay's assumptions on photovoltaics have turned out to be ludicrously pessimistic. In his calculations of land required, he assumed mass market modules were 10% efficient and expensive modules 20%; as of 2018, a mass market module is 17.2% efficient [Jiang *et al.*, 2018], with expensive modules at 22%. While economics was not MacKay's focus, he dismissed PV largely because other sources pegged cost at around 571 pounds/MWh; the last (and as of late 2018, only) solar tender in the UK was won at 79.2 pounds/MWh, in 2015, by developer Lightsource. In 2017, Greece generated 7.2% of its electricity from PV, Germany 6.1% and Italy 8.5% without any of these countries being noticeably short of space for further solar panels. Wind turbines have made similar advances; a typical wind turbine built in the 1990s in Germany had capacity of about 500 kW, while a new turbine in 2018 is likely to be at least 2.5 MW, and achieves a significantly higher capacity factor as well, through more reliable power electronics, better maintenance, and simply having the blades higher up where the wind is stronger.

Dr Ajay Gambhir, a Senior Research Fellow at the Imperial College London Grantham Institute for Climate Change and the Environment, suspects that land use will not be the limiting factor for solar. "From a physical perspective, photovoltaics is a much more efficient way of converting sunlight into power than is photosynthesis and harvesting of biomass", he points out. Research by NREL scientists concluded that there was potential on US rooftops alone for 731 GW of PV, or enough to produce about 25% of current US electricity sales, while covering 28% of small roofs [Elmore *et al.*, 2018]. Similar studies in other countries suggest that there is plenty of rooftop and land that is marginal for other uses to generate a large amount of the country's electricity demand. In some places, agriculture or wildlife habitat can be combined with solar panels, or solar can be used on lakes and reservoirs, which also reduces evaporation.

Another ground for reasonably hoping that MacKay was too pessimistic is that he may have underestimated the extent to which we can reduce our total energy use in transport, electricity and gas.

## 22.2. Electrification of Transport

Electrification of transport is now happening. About 1.1 million passenger electric vehicles were sold in 2017 and 1.5 million expected in 2018, up from 448,000 in 2015 and 288,000 in 2014 [Rybczynska, 2018]. This is still less than 1% of global new car sales, but the rate of acceleration is encouraging and new models get steadily more attractive and affordable, with the batteries benefitting from the same experience curve-based improvement process as solar panels and semiconductor chips.

Dr Ajay Gambhir says, "The low-hanging fruit now — and I wouldn't have said this 10 years ago — is the electrification of light duty transport. There's real momentum around reducing cost and increasing energy density [the weight of batteries needed to carry a certain amount of energy], range anxiety [the fear of being stranded between charging points, or of having to stop inconveniently often to recharge] is decreasing, and, to use a cliché, Tesla has made electric cars cool. Countries are also competing to electrify transport and eradicate the internal combustion engine, and with it the diseases of local air pollution such as pulmonary disease".

Do electric vehicles help reduce carbon dioxide emissions? Yes; it is significantly more efficient to generate electricity by burning fuel in a power plant than in an internal combustion engine, plus most power grids get at least some of their electricity from low carbon sources like hydroelectricity, nuclear, solar and wind. For example, a 2018 Canadian study concluded that a typical electric vehicle (a Nissan Leaf) started to save carbon emissions after 30,000 km relative to a similar-sized gasoline vehicle if charged with clean electricity, and 60,000 km even if charged from the relatively dirty Alberta power grid [Argue *et al.*, 2018]. Most cars are driven for at least 150,000 km in their lifetime.

The rise of electric vehicles also means that we can expect there to be a large number of batteries in the future energy system, which could with a little cleverness be charged only at times when solar and wind generation is high, and could even be discharged for short periods to support the grid (see Chapter 23). This would help balance a grid with a large amount of renewable power output, as well as ensuring that the cars are being driven almost entirely on clean energy.

Gambhir's research includes marginal abatement cost curves (MACCs or MAC curves), a way to compare the cost of reducing a tonne of carbon dioxide emission from different sources, with the goal of identifying the easiest wins. "We used to make MAC curves showing electric vehicles at about $400/tonne, near the top of the MAC curve" he says. "But that has changed". One of his papers from 2015 (Figure 22.2) illustrates both the principle of MAC curves and the difficulties in producing a forecast that continues to look accurate for long enough to be published in an academic journal, given how rapidly costs are falling. It also shows a typical feature of MAC curves, that some methods to reduce carbon emissions have negative cost, i.e. they save money. Often these options include energy efficiency measures, which do save money but are difficult to implement quickly in large volumes.

While currently many electric vehicle sales are subsidised, this is often driven by a desire to reduce local air pollution in major cities,

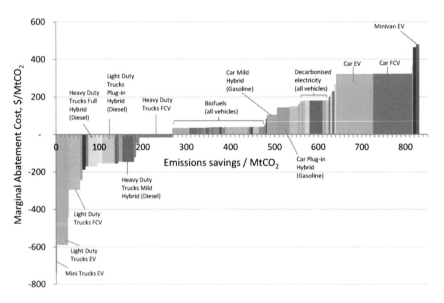

Figure 22.2.   Outdated marginal abatement cost curve (MAC curve) forecast of China's road transport sector in 2050 [Gambhir *et al.*, 2015]. All cost figures in 2010 US dollars; EV = Electric Vehicle; FCV = Fuel Cell Vehicle; Colours/shading for clarity only (i.e. different abatement options are not colour-coded).

*Source*: Reprinted with permission from Elsevier.

a problem that is unlikely to go away before a significant proportion of the transport fleet is electrified.

## 22.3. Efficiency in the Energy Sector

Thirdly, there is considerable progress in making developed-world lifestyles more energy-efficient. UK regulator Ofgem's 2017 State of the Energy Market report pointed out that UK households reduced their average consumption of both electricity and gas by about 20% between 2006 and 2016, largely due to more energy-efficient electrical devices and upgrading of the building stock with cavity wall insulation and condensing boilers. Light-emitting diodes (LEDs) for interior lamps, for example, use less than a quarter of the energy of the incandescent bulbs that preceded them, and last much longer while supplying the same amount of light. There is further potential for better insulation to reduce energy use for both heating and cooling, in cool and hot climates, respectively.

Energy demand in India and south-east Asia is still rising rapidly as people enjoy rising living standards, but in China and some Latin American countries, the demand for electricity at least has stagnated despite (by some metrics) rising standards of living. Brazil cancelled a renewable energy auction at the end of 2016 simply because it did not need any more electricity. China cancelled some 120 GW of planned coal fired power plants at the same time, admitting that realistic projections of growth do not require them.

The most plausible plan to put the human race on a trajectory to stabilising the greenhouse gas content of the atmosphere, while giving every human the standard of living we currently expect in the West, is to clean up the electricity mix, and at the same time electrify everything, while making efficiency improvements everywhere in our economy. We are a long, long way away from this — but the technology to do so is beginning to be available.

Dr Ajay Gambhir concludes that "My biggest worry is real world feasibility. It is very easy to produce a [modelled] scenario that would produce a 1.5°C temperature change, which would have been absurd to say about 10 years ago". He suggests however that papers presenting such scenarios are being produced due to demand for the papers, rather than necessarily because the scenarios are likely on current evidence.

Flying around the globe as freely as we do today may never be sustainable, although you never know — a Swiss solar-powered plane, called SolarImpulse, managed to carry a single human passenger in steps around the world in 2016. At present, avoiding flying wherever possible is probably the most worthwhile climate measure an individual can take.

## 22.4. The Nuclear Option

It's possible to argue that we do not have to reduce energy use at all, and we could simply electrify everything to cut carbon emissions, if we just expanded our use of nuclear power.

Historically the groups which have campaigned for renewables (Friends of the Earth, Greenpeace, the German green party) have also campaigned against nuclear. In addition, most owners of US nuclear power plants have historically also operated coal-fired plants and so have not committed to lobbying for nuclear on grounds of averting climate change. (This may change — for example Exelon, the largest nuclear plant operator in the US, sold or retired its last coal-fired power plant in February 2017. Perhaps there will now be a more concerted effort from US nuclear lobbyists to attack coal rather than renewables).

It remains difficult for many environmental groups to truly embrace nuclear power, even when it does not come bundled with coal. There is no doubt that high levels of radioactivity are dangerous and that nuclear waste needs careful handling. At least 58 people died as a direct result of the disaster in April 1986 at Chernobyl, Ukraine — and it could easily have been much worse. The accident was due to human error, and nuclear advocates point out that with today's much better safety procedures, it should never happen again. Nobody died as a direct result of radiation from the Fukushima accident in March 2011, although there are plausible reports that over 2,000 people died as a result of unnecessary evacuation. Nuclear critics point to human nature as Exhibit A for why accidents like Chernobyl, or worse, could easily happen again.

On the other hand, climate change would have progressed considerably further than it has today without nuclear, which emits practically no carbon dioxide (arguments about which non-fossil energy source has lower lifecycle emissions depend heavily on assumptions, and are pretty pointless when compared to the much higher emissions of any fossil source). In 1973 (the earliest date for which the IEA published data in its World Energy Statistics 2017) nuclear produced 203 TWh of electricity worldwide (3.3% of generation, versus 20.9% for hydro) and grew from there, peaking in 2006 at 2,660 TWh. Nuclear represented 10.6% of total global electricity production in 2015, while solar is only about 2% globally as of 2018. (It's surprisingly difficult to find precisely comparable statistics for the same recent year.)

The effects of nuclear power on carbon dioxide emissions are very clear. France, which made a huge national strategic push for nuclear in the 1970s during an oil price shock (and founded the International Energy Agency at the same time), generated 72% of its electricity from this source in 2016, and in consequence shines like a beacon on any emissions map of Europe, usually emitting less than 10% of the carbon dioxide per kWh that its neighbour Germany produces. Ontario is similar, producing 58% of its 2015 electricity from nuclear (plus 23% from hydro, with no coal at all). German carbon dioxide emissions from energy fell only 7% between 2005 and 2016 despite huge growth in renewables, according to data from the Umwelt Bundesamt, largely due to less nuclear generation. Nuclear plants can also be used to supply heat for entire districts as well as electricity, turning what is normally a waste product into something extremely useful.

Nonetheless, nuclear is an industry in retreat, at least in the West. Germany plans to close all its reactors by 2022. France plans to phase out nuclear in its generation fleet, although the timeline is unclear and keeps changing. The Olkiluoto 3 reactor in Finland is expected to be completed in late 2019, 10 years behind schedule and three times over budget. A number of US nuclear power plants are being decommissioned ahead of schedule.

Although the Fukushima accident in 2011 was the trigger for a widespread move away from state support of nuclear, the more recent problems for nuclear have been mainly economic. In the US, a note by BNEF in June 2017 [Steckler, 2017] estimated that 55% of US nuclear power plants were not making a profit due to wholesale power prices of just $20–30/MWh. The low price of natural gas in the US due to increased shale gas extraction is part of the reason for this.

One feature of nuclear is that it has low operational cost, once spread over a large number of MWh (and nuclear plants have in the past typically run above 80% capacity factor, so 1 GW of nuclear power produces roughly as much energy as 4 GW of PV or 2 GW of onshore wind farms). The BNEF 2017 study pegged typical US nuclear operating costs at $35/MWh. However, the capex is extremely high, so if the nuclear plant does not achieve high load factors (for example, because the power is not needed), the economics are poor. Nuclear plants do not save any fuel by not running for a few hours, like a fossil fuel plant would.

Integrating nuclear with renewables, or running a grid on a very high percentage of nuclear baseload generation, is possible but not trivial. The process of shifting nuclear plant output up and down ('ramping') is quite complex compared with the 'stop feeding it fuel' approach for fossil generation, or the 'use the inverter to move the system away from its optimal voltage-current configuration' approach for solar. Reducing the output of a nuclear power plant is called 'poisoning the reactor' with elements which absorb neutrons and hence slow down the chain reaction, and it's easier to ramp down one reactor a lot than all reactors a little (I have been told that the term for changing the output of a nuclear fleet is 'playing the piano', with power plants as keys. If this isn't true, it should be). France uses a lot of its nighttime nuclear electricity generation to heat water for daytime use, rather than reducing output from its reactors (a technique that would also work to make use of short-term overproduction from renewable energy).

There is also potential for new nuclear fission technologies to be smaller, safer and cheaper. Small Modular Reactors, for example, are a scaled-down model under 300 MW similar to those used in nuclear fsubmarines. However, these are estimated to be still at least 10 years away from commercial viability, and there may be some popular resistance to a mini nuclear power plant in every village.

There's an unfortunate tendency for both nuclear and renewable energy advocates to suggest that their way is the only way to supply energy. I think we need all the tools in the box to combat climate change, and that certainly closing existing nuclear plants ahead of schedule is a bad idea.

# Chapter 23

# The Challenges of Intermittency, and Possible Solutions

In late February 2018, the UK was in the grip of an extreme weather system called the 'Beast from the East'. This was a period of intense cold and snow across the country, which is usually protected by the warmth of the Gulf Stream ocean current, and has infrastructure designed for a generally clement climate.

I was by coincidence in the UK at the time, and had breakfast near the office with some colleagues, chatting and pointing out the new electric London buses passing on the road. Gas analyst John Twomey arrived late and in a manic mood; the UK National Grid had issued warnings about a deficit in the gas supply. This was particularly low because the Rough storage facility, a depleted gas field off the coast of Yorkshire used to store about nine days' worth of UK gas supply, had been retired the summer before. There were also technical problems on a gas interconnector with the Netherlands. The UK relies on gas for a significant amount of its heating and electricity, and the cold weather meant that heating demand was very high. "It's so exciting!" said Twomey, with the delight of an expert about to learn something new. "We're about to see what happens to the UK power grid in a crisis!" And he ran off to help the power team write something up for our clients about it [Annex *et al.*, 2018].

In fact, the Beast from the East did not bring the UK power system crashing down (although it did cause havoc on the train network). Prices for gas shot up fivefold in a week, and since power is the most flexible

171

source of demand for gas, generation from combined cycle gas turbines fell 30% week-on-week.

The shortfall was made up by wind and coal. One unusual thing about the Beast from the East compared with most UK cold weather systems was that it was very windy, enabling the UK's wind farms to produce about 25% of the country's power throughout. However, coal power output also increased 79% in the week. Solar was almost no help as it was winter, and with a whole week of extreme conditions to deal with, any battery capability would have been severely depleted. To put it bluntly, if the coal had not been supported by government capacity payments, the country might have had to choose between light and heat. All of the UK's coal plants are scheduled to shut down by 2025.

Any discussion of making solar and wind a major part of our energy supply generally deals with how we handle intermittency, i.e. what we do when the sun goes down and the wind does not blow. Unfortunately, I don't have the final answer to this, but I hope to show in this chapter that it is not an insurmountable obstacle to a very high level of renewables on the grid. Human ingenuity put a man on the moon, brought electricity to nearly every house in the West, and put a remote communication device in nearly every human hand. I cannot believe our species needs to keep burning fossil fuels until we roast ourselves, simply because of a minor timing issue.

The first and simplest answer is always 'batteries'. Batteries do have the potential to solve several problems at once (see Table 23.1), and are getting much cheaper with wider deployment in electric vehicles. Battery prices are still all over the place, but BNEF estimates that an average price for lithium ion packs in 2017 was $209/kWh, down from $599/kWh in 2013. The per-kWh price is complicated because of course batteries are measured by how much energy they can store (as well as by their peak discharge rate in kW). They lose capacity as they are used, but can be charged and discharged thousands of times. Thanks to the reduced prices, batteries are in the early stage of deployment at grid scale — for example, a UK auction in December 2016 awarded payments to 501 MW of various batteries, to stabilise the UK grid. On the island of Kauai in Hawaii, where the cost of diesel generation is estimated to be over $150/MWh, battery and solar company Tesla has contracted to deliver baseload (24 h) power from a solar plant and a battery for $139/MWh. This is made more

Table 23.1. Summary of intermittency problems and potential solutions.

| Challenge of very high renewables penetration | Potential solutions | Level of fundamental technical challenge at today's technology level |
|---|---|---|
| Distribution grid unable to handle reverse flows of power from houses to the grid. | Build stronger distribution grid as Germany has done. Add distributed batteries when they become cheap enough. | Low — just requires investment. |
| Minute-to-minute fluctuations in renewable generation causing grid frequency problems. | Batteries. Demand response (i.e. turning off loads like freezers and AC for minutes). | Low — requires some investment. |
| Day-to-night fluctuations. | A mixture of renewables in the grid (e.g. solar, wind, hydro). Pumped hydro or compressed air energy storage. Larger amounts of the batteries used to regulate grid frequency. Time of day power pricing to encourage power users to change their use patterns. Long-range transmission infrastructure. | Medium — will be more expensive for some countries than others. |
| Seasonal variation in solar or wind generation. | Mixture of renewables in the grid (generally, wind and hydro generate more in the winter). Long-range transmission infrastructure. Chemical storage of energy (e.g. making hydrogen in summer for winter use). Emergency power plants, for example diesel generators or open cycle gas turbines. | High — transmission lines are politically fraught, new wind and hydro plants can take years of seeking planning permission, emergency power plants would still use fuel. |
| Transmission grid unable to transfer energy from renewable energy plants to load centres. | More transmission grid. Simply accepting curtailment of renewable generation at exceptional times. | Medium — only costs money. |

feasible by the fact that Hawaii is near the equator, so day and night are nearly the same length all year.

In any case, the problems of intermittency are different on different timescales.

## 23.1. Minutes and Hours

Solar generation ramps sharply and falls quickly over a period of hours even on a uniformly sunny day (Figure 23.1), which presents problems because most gas and coal plants are not designed to ramp up and down so quickly. Between 8:30 and 9:30 am, the PV output in Germany on this day rises by 6.8 GW, or roughly 10% of Germany's entire average power consumption. This means the equivalent of two or three gas plants being shut off in that hour, or more likely the entire fleet of gas plants turned down a little. Which is fine, while you have an entire fleet of gas plants to turn down, as in Germany today.

This is at least predictable, and does save fuel being burned during the day, but the operators of the fossil power plants lose revenue and may shut

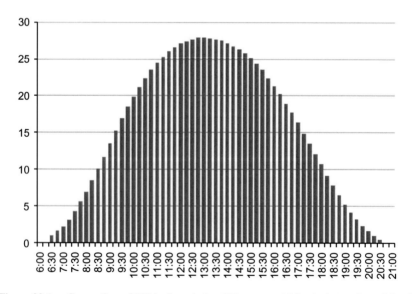

Figure 23.1.   Generation of PV in the whole of Germany at 15-min intervals on May 8, 2016 (GW), from SMA Solar Technology's website monitoring tool.

down if they stop making enough money to cover the upkeep cost of the plant. In a perfect market, some of the gas plants would shut down, and the spot market prices after dark would go sky-high, compensating gas generators which had kept their plants online for the lost profit. If electricity prices rose to thousands of dollars per MWh, it might also be worth exploring other options, such as 'demand response' (turning off power-consuming devices such as industrial freezers or office heating for minutes or hours, until the power prices fell again) or batteries to store electricity.

Perhaps unfortunately, most regulators dislike power prices in the thousands of dollars per MWh, and try other solutions such as offering the plants 'capacity payments' to stay open. This means that they are paid to be available even if they are not needed. Capacity payments cost money, and may also discourage adoption of demand response and batteries by reducing the incentive to do so. Michael Liebreich argued in January 2017 that, "simply layering on a capacity market is the wrong response: creating guaranteed demand for obsolete technologies has never ended well", and the argument for free power markets seems compelling. BNEF's power analysts, however, are not all on board with this market fundamentalist approach, mainly because power generation is a natural monopoly and therefore needs to be carefully regulated to function as a market at all. The irony of a market needing to be heavily regulated to enable free trade is not lost on my power market colleagues.

The problem with solar is often even worse on the minute-by-minute level for individual systems, where weather systems can cause output to swing up and down on timeframes which are more difficult to predict (Figure 23.2). The output on a cloudy day is likely to be predictable across a whole country, but local fluctuations can be considerable.

If the sun goes behind a cloud, the output from solar panels on the grid drops instantly, which causes the grid voltage to drop. The grid responds by dropping the frequency of the alternating current slightly, which can destroy sensitive devices, interrupt critical processes and even cause other solar inverters — which work at grid frequency — to cut out, which takes more solar off. This can be a vicious circle ending with blackout. It has been pretty much fixed in Germany and other developed markets by requiring inverters to have 'ride-through' capabilities, i.e. not

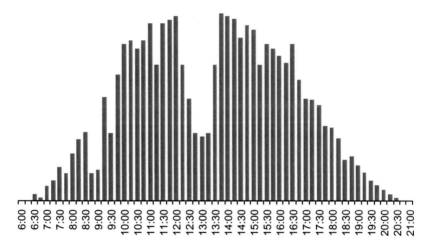

Figure 23.2.   Output of a hypothetical PV system at 15-min intervals on a day with intermittent cloud cover, as proportion of capacity.

go offline just because the grid frequency fluctuated briefly, so such a fluctuation does not crash the entire grid. There are also ways to provide frequency support; batteries and flywheels (devices that store kinetic energy by spinning fast) are well suited to producing energy for a short time to support the grid frequency. There are already market-based mechanisms to pay for frequency response services, and we are starting to see multi-MW batteries on the grid being paid to provide these services. However, they do not have the capacity to either charge or discharge for hours at a time.

Demand response would also work at this scale; nobody would even notice if all the refrigerators in a city stopped cooling for 15 min. In Texas, which has a surprising amount of wind turbines — the Electric Reliability Council of Texas (ERCOT) reported wind and solar to have supplied 18% of its electricity in 2017 — grid operators have been known to literally phone major factories and offer them money to shut down for periods when the wind output looks likely to be lower than was forecast a few days earlier. Obviously, as this becomes a more frequent event, it is likely that this process will be automated and contracted, and run more smoothly.

Most of these cost money — even the owners of the refrigerators probably need some compensation for a utility being able to remotely operate their device. However, they are technically completely feasible, and could probably be achieved with minimal disruption.

Incidentally, this is why the 'smart home' falls under the subject of clean energy. A smart home, where all devices are online and can be remotely controlled, could in theory support the power grid without causing the owner the slightest inconvenience. However, if smart homes do become ubiquitous, security will be a priority and bugs will need to be fixed, because nobody wants to have their heating hacked or to be unable to make tea because the internet is down. At present, it is difficult to see smart homes offering owners value worth taking this risk for, but if solar is practically free in the daytime this may change. Early adopters of smart homes are generally doing it for fun or security, or out of curiosity.

## 23.2. Seasons

The really tough problem for a high penetration of solar in countries that are not on the equator is seasonal variation in output, and extreme conditions such as the Beast from the East. PV in Germany produces roughly 17 times as much energy on the sunniest day of the year (usually in May or June) as on the least sunny (usually in January or February). Even if we had batteries that could store a night's worth of power, charging them from solar power in the winter would be economically unreasonable — the batteries would cycle only once a year, thus would need to be simply enormous and would be incredibly expensive.

Can we store summer solar power at all? Not easily. Proposed solutions include warming large lakes of underground water, or blocks of rock, in summer, drawing the heat for use in winter. Alternatively, we could use summer electricity to make a chemical fuel. Hydrogen is a common example, but the hydrogen molecule is very small and escapes from confinement very easily, so a heavier hydrocarbon might be desirable. Hydrogen can already be pumped into the German gas grid at low levels, but would present safety and leakage issues at high penetrations. Fuel cell cars, which could run directly on hydrogen, do not solve the hydrogen storage problem and currently lag far behind electric vehicles in market take-up. These options are in the realm of the improbable, for now, although BNEF estimates a cost of hydrogen and fuel cells for seasonal electricity load shifting at 244 euros/MWh [Curry *et al.*, 2017] — expensive, but not incredibly so. The really big problem with making hydrogen by electrolysis of water from solar and wind power is that electrolysis equipment is expensive to build. This means that even if the price of solar and wind-generated electricity is zero at times, it needs to be so for a high proportion of the year in order to pay off the upfront investment. Like power plants, electrolysis plants need to run a lot to amortise the capex.

An obvious choice is to have a good mix of solar, wind and hydroelectric power in the grid — since generally the less sunny it is in a season, the more it rains. This may well lead to rational governments and regulators in the northern hemisphere being willing to pay much more for wind power than for solar power in future, and also to approve new hydroelectric dams. On March 8, 2017, the Welsh planning office approved the UK's first hydroelectric facility for 30 years, the Glyn Rhonwy Pumped Storage Scheme.

Connecting a country's power grid with a neighbouring one can also be a powerful tool in integrating renewables. According to the UK Energy Research Centre, Germany hit 45.5 GW of renewable generation for a brief period in May 2016, against instantaneous power demand of 45.8 GW; since the country also had 7.7 GW of fossil fuel capacity online, the excess was exported to Germany's many neighbours. (Not all are entirely happy with this, incidentally, and there have been disputes over the use of Germany's interconnection on the Czech border.) Power lines are being planned north to Scandinavia, where winter hydropower is plentiful. Another option for Europe would be to run a power line towards the equator, to countries which are sunny even in winter (the Middle East actually has a low period in power consumption in winter, as the need for air conditioning is reduced, so it might happen to export solar power if it built enough to supply summer demand). This is technically practical, but would leave us reliant heavily on the Middle East for energy, a situation with an element of *deja vu*.

A final option, if we got to a very high penetration of renewables in the grid which could cause major blackouts in unusual weather conditions — for example, a low wind situation in winter, expected for a week a year or so — we could build emergency power plants, either diesel or open cycle gas turbines. Open cycle gas turbines (OCGTs) are very inefficient at consuming gas compared with the more usual closed cycle gas turbines, but like diesel generators they are cheap to build and quick to start up. These allow a country to run at a generally very high level of renewables, and kick in if strictly needed. Most island grids already use a lot of diesel, because on a small grid demand is difficult to predict and match. Neither diesel nor OGCTs are at all clean, but perhaps if they only run occasionally, that'll be okay.

These solutions are not mutually exclusive — indeed, having a large number of batteries in the grid solves several different problems, particularly if they are embedded in the distribution grid (not necessarily in households — they could be in villages or estates) provided they are under the control of the grid operator. Likewise, better and larger transmission grids solve several problems. Some advocates are keen on the idea of individual households going offgrid, but it is my opinion that we built the grid for a reason. It is much cheaper and more efficient to aggregate load, generation and storage than it is to overbuild capacity for individual houses, or indeed countries. While offgrid households may make sense in countries which have not yet built a grid, it would be a shame to throw away the billions of dollars' worth of grid infrastructure to duplicate it with smaller systems.

Analysis of the effect of any generator on the grid needs to be probabilistic, weighing up the probability of each generator being available when needed (which even for a coal or gas plant, is not 1; unplanned outages happen even to the best plants). Most analyses to date (for example in the 200 journal papers reviewed by the UK Energy Research Centre in its Intermittency Report, published February 2017) start with an existing grid configuration and calculate the cost and effect of adding further renewables to it. These usually conclude that the cost and effect range widely, depending on factors such as the flexibility of the other power plants in the grid, the times when the grid's power demand is highest, the strength of the transmission and distribution grid to move electricity around the system, and the interconnection with other countries — but that these costs are not unbearable at current penetration levels (up to about 40% of renewables in electricity supply). It is reasonably clear how we can get to 50%, 60% or 70% of renewables in a country's electricity supply, and once we have done that we will have much more knowledge, experience and technology to figure out how to get to 80% and eventually phase out fossil fuels altogether.

That is, unless civilisation collapses and we lose all our hard-won technical expertise first. Or unless every country pursues a rigid energy independence goal, insisting on owning power capacity within its own borders for every eventuality. This would be turning our backs on the reason we built a power grid in the first place: to aggregate load and make it more predictable, and to make generation flexible and resilient to incidents. As a species, we're not going anywhere else fast, so we'd better work together to keep this planet livable.

# Chapter 24

# What Next for Solar?

Every year, standard crystalline silicon gets a bit cheaper or performs a bit better. In 2018 alone, we have been surprised by the rapid expansion of bifacial modules, which give you a bit more energy just by using glass on the back instead of an opaque sheet. We have also been surprised by the rise of floating solar, especially in Korea and Japan, which can overcome land constraints while reducing evaporation from reservoirs. The march of progress is far from done. Human civilization is still in the 'shallow decarbonisation' phase where solar is nowhere near fundamental limits of what it can supply, as most of the grid runs on fossil fuels. Deep decarbonisation, taking us to zero net emissions, is barely even on the technological radar, although Spain and California have targets to run on 100% clean energy by 2050 and 2045, respectively.

However, solar is already cheaper on a per-MWh basis in many sunny countries than natural gas, and cheaper per MWh for households in many countries than the retail price of electricity. There's the idea of a 'tipping point' much discussed by enthusiasts over the decades. The idea of this is that once solar no longer needs subsidies, demand for it will suddenly explode.

This probably will not actually happen. Solar has been exploding for the past 10 years because of subsidies. The actual economics of solar are now worse in many places than before, despite the fall in costs, because subsidies are being removed. That is fine; often the subsidies were higher than they needed to be to reward people for building. But for people and organisations, there is no reason to rush to build large-scale solar to feed electricity into grids, or to put solar on rooftops, when you are not trying to meet a deadline to secure a subsidy. It's fairly obvious that costs will only come down, and build in some markets, such as Australia and Germany, continues with very little support.

The places where solar will change lives in the next 10 years are countries which need more power. India, many Latin American countries, much of south-east Asia and Africa have a rapacious demand for ongrid power and excellent sunshine. In most of these countries, the energy grid is built more or less by central government planning, so holding competitive tenders to add more power capacity is the standard procedure and adding solar to the options is no big deal.

It is not always easy to do business in these countries; corruption can make it difficult for the experienced Western companies to set up contracts and financing the way they would like, and political unrest, terrorism and war threaten solar plant revenues as much as they threaten people. Local companies lack experience in building solar plants (which is not rocket science, but is not trivial either) and international companies may reasonably be distrusted by governments. Nigeria plans a major initiative to build several GW of solar, but this has been delayed some years by the need to reward Nigerian solar project developers who have done some work towards projects, while not rewarding them with the very high prices offered years ago before global solar technology prices dropped — and the government appears to be paralysed by this dilemma, as well as possibly waiting for even lower prices.

There may be simple physical problems with abruptly increasing a country's power supply. Norwegian developer Scatec Solar has built an 8.5 MW PV project in Rwanda, connecting it to the country's 150 MW power grid. Unfortunately, Rwanda frequently had such severe power supply problems that a quarter of the country at a time experienced planned electricity blackouts — and the design of grid-connected projects is such that the PV project had to stop supply to the grid while it goes down, for the first few years of the plant's operation (it has reportedly been improved). Undeterred, Scatec is also moving forward on securing finance for a 33 MW photovoltaic project in Mali, which will make a significant difference on a 500 MW grid. Honduras already gets 10.2% of its electricity from solar, as reported by state power company ENEE in January 2017 — and the power grid of Honduras is a whole 2 GW.

In places with a competitive power market, building new solar is not as simple as responding to a government tender. Historically, with spot power prices averaging $20–100/MWh depending on country, solar could compete. There are several solar projects built with this as a plan, notably the 53 MW Los Loros project developed by Solairedirect in Chile, mainly financed by development banks.

The problem with merchant solar power plants is one that should have been intuitively obvious even before 2015, but was not widely discussed because we could not imagine there being enough solar in the grid to make this a problem: solar plants all generate at the same time. Nearly exactly the same time, in fact, although there is a little difference in weather and longitude across a country. They are far more correlated than wind. The result is that they supply the grid, using the inexorable marginal cost logic described in Chapter 10, at the same time. In consequence, if the spot power market is working, the spot price crashes — and can hit zero, as it has already in certain parts of the power grid in Chile in a sunny hour.

A solar plant selling to a grid with a moderate amount of existing solar capacity will receive a much lower average power price than a gas plant, which might well minimise its output between 11 am and 2 pm every day, and ramp up to supply power in the evening. BloombergNEF analysis of California in February 2017, a market where historically sunny hours have been high-price hours due to the use of air conditioning, found that the average price for a solar plant selling entirely to the spot market in 2016 would have been just $24/MWh, compared with $34/MWh for a gas plant running all the time [Nelson *et al.*, 2017]. In reality, the gas plant could also pick its hours to run only when margins were good.

Is this unfair? Well, not really, if you believe the spot market is a reasonable way to allocate resources (and fundamentally I do). There's no point in building more capacity which by definition generates most when it is not needed. The gas plants receive higher prices in the evenings, which keeps their operating margins ('spark spreads' — the difference between the price of fuel and maintenance, and the price of the electricity) positive. If the prices fell, some gas plants would go offline, and the prices would pick up again or the lights would go off.

When I started writing this book in 2014, it seemed completely unrealistic to expect enough batteries to be added to the grid to make a difference to the midday depression in the price of solar. As of 2018, it is still not happening in bulk, but there are a few utility-scale batteries on the grid, such as Tesla's in South Australia, which do store solar power for later. This is no longer a ridiculous option for shifting daytime generation to cover the evening peak, although it feels like there have to be cheaper ways to do it.

Electric vehicle sales also continue to grow, and it would be a relatively simple matter to make sure these are plugged in when their drivers get to work, but start charging only when the sun gets high. This would help flatten power demand and power prices across the day.

One of the effects of cheap solar that Western consumers will notice in the next 10 years will be that their power bills become more complicated. Utilities will offer cheaper power during peak sun hours, or even power tariffs that change minute-by-minute depending on the sun and the wind level. You may be offered money to let the utility control when your freezer chills or your immersion heater heats. If you drive an electric vehicle, you are already offered special power tariffs as utilities try to secure you as a high-use customer and also use the flexibility of your vehicle to make the power grid more resilient. If you live in a developed country, your life will probably not change much otherwise in the next decade.

Deep decarbonisation — getting to zero net emissions — is difficult even for energy (never mind for agriculture, which is likely to become a major problem as climate change worsens). The main challenge not addressable by today's technologies is the risk of extreme conditions like a week of bitterly cold, still weather in northern Europe. If we have electrified everything, including heat, this would coincide with exceptionally high and inflexible demand for electricity. Climate change will also hurt electricity production in unpredictable ways; smoke from 2018's wildfires in California significantly reduced solar production, and in the same summer, some European nuclear plants reduced output because the cooling water was too hot. For deep decarbonisation, we might have to look at expensive and inefficient options like hydrogen, or storing summer heat in a lake of molten salt under Rotterdam.

The human race learns by trying things, and high and widespread penetration of solar power is yet to be tried. Over the next 10 years, it is obvious that we will be trying it. We will see more rooftop solar panels in developed countries, while progress is steadily made in managing the power generation and consumption system in these countries to get more value out of the fact that power for a few hours around noon on a sunny day is very cheap, or even essentially free. At the same time, we will see countries such as Mali, Rwanda, Ethiopia and Zambia begin to build substantial amounts, boosting their economies without a concurrent rise in carbon emissions. As they start to build grids, factories, business models and infrastructure based around cheap midday power, rather than building an economy based on coal or gas, we will hopefully continue to learn lessons that will enable a transition to a sustainable future.

# References

Annex, M., Gandolfo, A., Knight, T., Marquina, D., Olsen, J., Twomey, J. and Rooze, J. (2018). Winter Storm Tests U.K. Security of Supply, *BloombergNEF*, Insight note 18157.

Argue, C., Davis, R. and Poovanna, P. (2018). Supplementary Information, Environmental Life Cycle Assessment of Electric Vehicles in Canada, *Institute for Research on Public Policy*.

Banerjee, A., Karlan, D. and Zinman, J. (2015). Six Randomized Evaluations of Microcredit: Introduction and Further Steps, *American Economic Journal: Applied Economics*, 7 (1), pp. 1–21.

Bromley, H., L'Ecluse, C., Jiang, Y., Radoia, P., Swarbreck, J. and Wang, X. (2018). 3Q 2018 PV Market Outlook, *BloombergNEF*, Insight note 19127.

Bullard, N., Chase, J., d'Avack, F. and Wu, X. (2008). PV Market Outlook Q4 2008, *BloombergNEF*, Insight note 978.

Chase, J. (2010). Thin-film Silicon at the Sharp End, *BloombergNEF*, Insight note 2135.

Chase, J., Chatterton, R., Grace, A., Giannakopoulou, E., Goldie-Scot, L., Harries, T., Henbest, S., Kimmel, M., Lu, S., Rooze, J. and Turner, A. (2018). BloombergNEF New Energy Outlook 2018, *BloombergNEF*, Insight note 18819.

Curry, C., Goldie-Scot, L., Hsiao, I. and Wilshire, M. (2017). Hydrogen as a source of grid flexibility, *BloombergNEF*, Insight note 16581.

De La Tour, A., Glachant, M. and Ménière, Y. (2013). Predicting the costs of photovoltaic solar modules in 2020 using experience curve models. *Energy*, 62(C), 341–348.

Elmore, R., Phillips, C., Gagnon, P., Margolis, R. and Melius, J. (2018). A data mining approach to estimating rooftop photovoltaic potential in the US, *Journal of Applied Statistics*, DOI: 10.1080/02664763.2018.1492525.

Feifel, C., Huber, S., Koch, M., Metzger. JW., Nover, J, Werner, JH. and Zapf-Gottwick, R. (2018). Schadstofffreisetzung aus Photovoltaik-Modulen: Abschlussbericht : Laufzeit: 01.09.2014-31.08.2017, University of Stuttgart, DOI: 10.2314/GBV:1020510552.

Frith, J. and Goldie-Scot, L. (2018). Will Cobalt and Lithium Shortages Slow EV Uptake? *BloombergNEF*, Insight note 18237.

Gambhir, A., Tse, LKC., Tong, D. and Martinez-Botas, R. (2015). Reducing China's road transport sector CO2 emissions to 2050: Technologies, costs and decomposition analysis, *Applied Energy*, DOI: 10.1016/j.apenergy.2015.01.018.

Gombar, V. (2017). Eight Development Banks Lent Clean Power $55 billion in 2016, *BloombergNEF*, Insight note 16747.

Hankey, R., Cassar, C., Liu, J., Wong, P. and Yildiz, O. (2018). *US Energy Information Administration Electric Power Monthly*, August 2018.

Hayim, L. (2018). PV O&M 2017: Providers Push Their Limits for Lower Prices, *BloombergNEF*, Insight note 18555.

Heck, S., Kaza, S. and Pinner, D. (2011). Creating value in the semiconductor industry, *McKinsey*.

Jiang, Y. and Wang, X. (2018). 2018 PV Manufacturing Overview: From Polysilicon to Module *BloombergNEF*, Insight note 19265.

Nelson, W. (2017). California Gas-fired Generation Worth 43% More than Solar in 2016 *BloombergNEF*, Insight note 15920.

Rybczynska, A. (2018). 2Q 2018 Global Electrified Transport Market Outlook, *BloombergNEF*, Insight note 18661.

Steckler, N. (2017). Half of U.S. Nuclear Power Plants are Underwater, *BloombergNEF*, Insight note 16511.

## Further Resources

Bazilian, M. and Roques, F. (2008). *Analytical Methods for Energy Diversity and Security,* 1$^{st}$ Ed. (Elsevier Science). — A textbook going into the mathematics of energy in much more detail.

RETScreen by Natural Resources Canada — software tools for various types of energy modelling, available free online.

# Key Terminology

**Capex (capital expenditure):** The cost to build or set up something.

**Cost of capital:** How much of a return (interest rate for debt, profit for equity) investors require to invest in a project. Confusingly, 'capital cost' is another term for capex, not cost of capital.

**Capacity:** In the context of energy, this usually refers to the peak power generation of a power plant, in W (or kW, MW etc). In the case of solar modules, this is defined as their output under standard conditions, 25°C temperature and 1000W per square metre of insolation. This insolation is roughly equivalent to noon on a sunny day in the south of Spain.

**Capacity factor:** How sunny it is. Usually defined as an equivalent percentage of the year the plant runs at full capacity, for example a UK solar plant might produce for the equivalent of 964 hours per year, or 11% (964 divided by the number of hours in the year).

**Equity index:** A portfolio of stocks selected to be representative of a market or sector (e.g. solar companies, companies listed on the Hong Kong stock exchange). The idea is that if investors want to put their money in this sector, they invest in an index rather than trying to pick companies that will be most successful.

**Initial Public Offering (IPO):** When a company first sells shares on a stock market, becoming a listed company. Usually, this is good news for the early investors in the company, as they can cash out.

**Insolation:** Sunniness. Also called solar radiation or irradiation. See capacity factor.

**Levelised Cost of Energy:** The price you have to pay someone to get them to build you an energy plant.

**Opex (operational expenditure):** The cost to keep something running (opex, like capex, is not exclusively an energy term).

**Return on Capital Employed (ROCE):** Mathematically, net operating profit divided by the money (capital) a company has put into an operation. A measure of how profitably a company is investing.

**Short selling:** The sale of a stock that does not belong to you (usually borrowed for a small fee). A bet that the stock price will go down, so you can buy the stock back at a lower price to return it.

**Yieldco:** A way to remove liquidity risk from projects which are not easily bought and sold. The revenues from the projects are bundled together and listed on a stock exchange, so investors can buy and sell the dividends. This makes solar project investment more attractive to firms which cannot invest directly in panels and fields. There are also wind, gas, transmission and other yieldcos. Suitable assets have predictable revenues and moderate returns.

# Index

Made in the USA
Middletown, DE
29 November 2023

44079578R00115